Continual Praise

The Key to Abundant Living

Dr. Jonathan Greer II

© Copyright 1994 — Jonathan Greer II

All rights reserved. This book is protected under the copyright laws of the United States of America. This book may not be copied or reprinted for commercial gain or profit. The use of short quotations or occasional page copying for personal or group study is permitted and encouraged. Permission will be granted upon request. Unless otherwise identified, Scripture quotations are from *The Living Bible* © 1971. Used by permission of Tyndale House Publishers, Inc. Wheaton IL 60189. All rights reserved.

Scriptures quotations marked (KJV) are taken from the King James Version of the Bible.

Scripture quotations marked (NIV) are taken from the Holy Bible, New International Version © 1973, 1978, 1984 by International Bible Society. Used by permission.

Take note that the name satan and related names are not capitalized. We choose not to acknowledge him, even to the point of violating grammatical rules.

Companion Press
P.O. Box 310
Shippensburg, PA 17257

"Good Stewards of the
Manifold Grace of God"

ISBN 1-56043-616-6

For Worldwide Distribution
Printed in the U.S.A.

Acknowledgment

I thank God for the Holy Spirit, who guided me and those individuals who labored with love, prayerful commitment, and practical advice, in the publication of this book.

Dedication

This book is affectionately dedicated to my loving parents, **Bishop and Mrs. Jonathan Greer, Sr.**, in appreciation for their love and inspiration in my life.

It is through their influence and instruction in the Word of God (the most precious of all knowledge), that I am able to keep my life in proper perspective—and praise God continually!

Psalm 150

Praise ye the Lord. Praise God in His sanctuary: praise Him in the firmament of His power.

Praise Him for His mighty acts; praise Him according to His excellent greatness.

Praise Him with the sound of the trumpet: praise Him with the psaltery and harp.

Praise Him with the timbrel and dance: praise Him with stringed instruments and organs.

Praise Him upon the loud cymbals: praise Him upon the high sounding cymbals.

Let every thing that hath breath praise the Lord. Praise ye the Lord.

Contents

	Foreword	vii
	Introduction	ix
Chapter 1	Don't Let a Day Go By Without Praise	1
Chapter 2	Let Your Praises Go Forth	15
Chapter 3	Freedom for the Troubled Heart	37
Chapter 4	A Prophecy of Encouragement	55
Chapter 5	Getting the Best of Yesterday	65
Chapter 6	Standing Firm in Praise	81
Chapter 7	Stand Firm in Faith	93
Chapter 8	There Is a Miracle at Your Fingertips	103
Chapter 9	God: Watchful and Faithful	117
Chapter 10	The Steadfast Love of the Lord Never Ceases	133
Chapter 11	God Causes You to Triumph	149
	Appendix	161

Foreword

I will praise the Lord no matter what happens ... Let all who are discouraged take heart. Let us praise the Lord together, and exalt His name (Psalm 34:1-3).

What is the essence of praise? Many Christians in these pessimistic times are looking for abundant life. *Continual Praise* answers these and other important questions about the attitude of praising God and the benefits of continual praise. This book will help the reader understand the spiritual concept of the *holy art* of praise and how *continual praise* is the key that unlocks the door to a more fruitful life.

Dr. Jonathan Greer II is very qualified to write this book because he possesses the heart of a worshiper, which allows him to share the thoughts contained in this book. He describes how praise is used as a catalyst against the negative forces of today's society and renders positive results. This book moves praise from a Sunday morning ritual to a continuous and vital part of our daily lives.

This book will motivate you to maintain an "attitude of gratitude" that will result in an abundant and victorious life. You will experience the transformation from being a victim to becoming a victor.

Not only of value to worship and praise leaders alike, *Continual Praise* will be of great use to every believer—Praise God!

> Pat Grigsby
> Praise Team Coordinator
> Cathedral of Faith
> Church of God in Christ
> Atlanta, Georgia

Introduction

Praise ye the Lord! This is how the psalmist ends Psalm 150, *Praise ye the Lord!* The cry of the psalmist was for himself, for those of his day, for those of the days that were to come and, yes, his words are for us today. It is time to praise the Lord!

From the first utterance of God's creation until today, there has never been a time when you should not praise God. And *now* is definitely the time to praise Him. You can begin right now. Take a moment, stop your reading, and enjoy yourself as you praise the Lord. Call your friends, call your neighbors, turn to your fellow worker. Ask them to join with you in praising God. You say you don't know how to praise God. Take heart and be of good cheer, for that is what this book is about, praising God. I want you to know the importance of praising God, and then I want you to demonstrate your understanding of its importance.

In times like these, the people of God need to know that praising God will be the most powerful weapon against the enemy. Do you know that you will experience your best days when you spend most of your time praising God? You will feel a lift in your spirit, a spring in your step, and the energy to accomplish your goals. On the other hand, your worst days will come when you focus mostly on the pressures of life first and start complaining about the problems before you. If more praise will bring more success, why don't you spend more time in praise?

Here is a fact you can count on: If you don't face your problems or whatever test you are going through with praise, you will have to go through that same course again. God will not allow you to go through a course complaining, and at the same time, let you pass the course. He wants you to pass the course without complaining, and if you don't pass, you will have to repeat the course. You will not get an "A" until you learn how to praise God in the midst of your trouble. When you go through the course praising God, God will bring you through the course by bringing more out of you.

Yes, praise will carry you through your trials, but more importantly, praise will keep you on course and help you finish the race. There are numerous benefits of praise. The following is a partial list.

Praise unlocks Heaven's portals, its gates, its doors. Praise benefits the soul. Praise causes doubt to cease. It leaves the sweetest peace. Praise breaks all bonds. Praise sets captives free. Praise lightens every burden by taking the weight out of every load. Praise is the master key. Praise changes circumstances. Praise establishes the heart. When praise becomes perpetual, praise is a holy art. When others are falling and fainting, praise keeps you going. When dark clouds are hanging over your head, praise will keep you going. Praise will keep you going when the winds of opposition blow against you.

To put it in the simplest of terms, praise works! Psalm 150 says, "Let every thing that hath breath praise the Lord!" Saints of old encouraged us, as the old traditional song says, to "praise Him in the morning, praise Him in the evening, praise Him when the sun goes down." Don't let a single day go by without praising the Lord.

Chapter 1

Don't Let a Day Go By Without Praise

Two Types of Saints

There are many deeply committed saints whose outlook on life always seems to be optimistic, cheerful, and bright. They smile more often than they frown. They can spot a silver lining around the darkest of clouds. Like Paul, they can see how their circumstances actually further the Kingdom (Phil. 1:12). They can detect the makings of an opportunity within the worst crisis. For these saints there is no hill too high and no valley too low. They rejoice in the events of their lives.

There are also saints who feel that sunny spirits are out of place in today's turbulent world. They peddle their gloom everywhere they go. It seems they are always complaining about the events that affect their lives. Often these gloom spreaders will go out of their way to tell you every negative thing that has happened to them. Moreover, they moan about those who don't understand their problems. They don't realize that the more they complain, the worse they will feel.

It is a simple truth that the more you focus on negative circumstances, the more frustrated you will become. Negative thinking produces discouragement and failure. You may ask, "How can such a difference exist between these two groups of saints?" The saints who always overcome their problems have learned how to achieve a rhythm of praise in their lives, blessing the Lord in all situations. Just as grumbling is a way of life for some, so is praise a way of life for others. Fortunately, you have a choice. You can learn how to praise God in the midst of your circumstances and, through praise, be raised above the circumstance. This happier way of life can be yours and mine even in these final troubled years of the twentieth century. With the breath of Pentecost ever present in the world, more Christians are turning to praise and, in the process, learning that praise is a part of God's call on their lives.

This call from Heaven to the saints of God encourages us to start praising God more. God is actually saying to the saints, "Praise Me more." Can you admit to having heard the call? Have you heard the voice of God? Many haven't heard because they refuse to listen. They are content to stoop to grumbling instead of standing up to praise. Yes, every day

God is saying to His people, "Praise ye the Lord." And we should express our praise to God because He is worthy of all praise. We should get our minds off of everything that stands in our way of praise. Hallelujah! Hallelujah! Hallelujah! Praise His name.

In Ephesians 1:14 in The Living Bible, Paul says that His Presence, which lives in us, is God's guarantee that He really will give us all that He promised. Furthermore, he says that the Spirit's seal upon us means that God has already purchased us and that He will bring us to Himself. God has chosen you, called you to Himself, put His Spirit in you, and guaranteed your position with Him. You didn't choose Him; He chose you. This is just one more reason for us to praise our glorious God.

In Luke's Gospel, the people take their cue from the disciples, who, after Jesus' ascension, returned to Jerusalem filled with joy. Each day they could be found in the Temple, praising the Lord.

And they worshiped Him, and returned to Jerusalem filled with mighty joy, and were continually in the Temple, praising God (Luke 24:52-53).

Like the disciples, it is time for the saints of today to continually praise the Lord. You must refuse to focus on anything that will take your mind away from the praise of God. When you are attending church, if you truly desire something from the service, you must get your mind on God and praise Him (see Ps. 100:4). The disciples weren't writing notes to each other or whispering to each other. They knew not to waste time while in God's sanctuary. The great joy that flowed through them drove them to express their appreciation for His mighty acts of grace with the sound of their praise toward Him.

If you are like me, God has been good to each of us personally. Would you agree to that? So, it is right to personalize our praise and make it uniquely our own expression. Praise promotes happiness. In fact, if you were to search for the shortest way to happiness and perfection, you would discover the right path by giving thanks and praise to God for everything that happens to you. Every success will be more of a success and every calamity will turn into a blessing if you will first think to praise God. In all things give thanks, for this is the will of God concerning you (see 2 Thess. 5:18). When I say "all things," I do not mean that you can pick and choose what to praise God for. I mean praise Him for "all things." The things the devil sends your way for evil, thank God for them, because God will turn them around for your good. Remember, everything is God's and everything is in His control.

Praise is also divine therapy that gladdens the spirit (see Prov. 17:22). This kind of therapy, the therapy of praise, clears the mind. Praise warms the heart and adds freshness and zest to your daily routine. Once you begin to offer this daily sacrifice of time for praise to God, you will also begin to experience the benefits of His many promises in return.

I can sense the excitement of the disciples as they continued steadfast in their praise of God. We need more saints who can get excited about praising God. Our praise of Him should not be simply because He helped us get a new job or showed us how to solve our financial problems. That is not to say that these personal victories should not cause us to praise God. But more important than all of the material things that God has given to us, He has given us Jesus. This is what we need to get excited about. Material victories are often temporary events that sometimes fade from memory. Jesus is a permanent victory that will fill us with joy and drive us to offer God our continual praise.

Praise as an Expression of Joy

Some people may have a problem expressing praise to God. Still, how do you think these same people would react if they received a million dollar gift? Would they calmly accept the gift without showing any emotion? Would they simply say, "Thank you very much"? More than likely they would burst out with shouts and screams, proclaiming their good fortune.

If they can declare their happiness when they win material things, then I can shout when Jesus gives me His love, joy, and peace. When the Lord God enters your heart, when you start knowing the Holy

Ghost is in you, you can't contain the joy. You have to express it. The Bible tells all of us in the land to make a joyful noise unto the Lord and to serve the Lord with gladness.

Continual Praise

Praise Him for the life that you live. Praise Him for the Jesus who lives in you. Some may hesitate to get as emotional as those early saints did. Still, they should be alert to the biblical summons to praise. The Book of Psalms introduces us to one person's enthusiastic resolution to praise. In Psalm 34:1, we see these words, "I will bless the Lord at all times..." Look at those last two words, *all times*. The word *all* does not allow any portion of time to be excluded. So, you praise whether you feel like it or not. You don't stop when things are not going your way. You don't stop because you don't feel like it. The psalmist concludes this verse by saying, "...His praise shall continually be in my mouth."

It is important that we understand that the psalmist, in using the word *mouth*, was not speaking of the lips or the physical mouth. In this case, the mouth is a metaphor for the spirit, for when you speak praise unto God, it is a spiritual statement. A word spoken from the spirit is not even in your physical mouth, and when this type of spiritual word is born, you can't help but praise God. Your mouth is on automatic pilot because your spirit is already soaring to the heavenly realm. You will begin to praise Him without being conscious of it. Hallelujah!

Have you ever been somewhere, perhaps on your job, and your hand goes up and you are not even aware that you raised it? Your mind, filled with earthly concerns, may have slowly turned to God and His greatness, goodness, and mercy. Suddenly, you are aware that your hand is raised and you say, "Oh, wait a minute. I forgot I'm on the job," and then you say aloud, "Thank You, Lord," or "Praise You, Jesus."

The Book of Hebrews calls upon Christians to keep praising God all of the time (see Heb. 13:15). With the help of Jesus, we will continually offer our sacrifice of praise to God by telling others of the glory of Jesus' name. Our continual praise is the fruit of our lips that acknowledges His name. Continual praise magnifies and glorifies His name, for there is no other name under heaven that is worthy of such praise, no other name whereby men are saved (see Acts 4:12).

Praise is like a fine diamond. It has many wonderful facets. Praise is an expression of approval, a positive affirmation. With our praise we laud, magnify, acclaim, honor, and glorify Him. Praise is an expression of a spirit filled with wonder and awe, with adoration and thanksgiving to God. Praise recognizes who He is and what He has done on our behalf.

In the Book of Psalms, we have an ancient record of the way God's chosen people praised Him. We can learn from their example. When you want to turn your mind from the problems of the day and prime your spirit to praise, turn to Psalm 34 and begin to read the words, first silently, and then ever so slowly allow the words of the psalm to rise up from inside and become a cry of joy unto God. "I will bless the Lord at all times: His praise shall continually be in my mouth" (Ps. 34:1). In saying these words over and over, you are glorifying God. You are before Him in awe of His majesty and you are adoring Him.

Now, substitute the name *Jesus* for the word *Lord*. Breathe out and concentrate on this wonderful name, Jesus. It is like opening a gift. You sigh, "Ahhhhh!" Marvel at the name as the praises pour forth from your spirit. Jesus is in your life. He is opening Himself to you in this pretty package God sent. When you open the package, you will find the presence of Jesus and you should sigh that sigh of wonder and joy.

It is time for us to stop taking Jesus for granted. It is time for us to put aside anything that might hinder our spirits and get excited about Him.

Let's look at more of Psalm 34, beginning with the first verse:

I will bless the Lord at all times: His praise shall continually be in my mouth. My soul shall make her boast in the Lord: the humble shall hear thereof, and be glad. O magnify the Lord with me, and let us exalt His name together (Psalm 34:1-3 KJV).

These words are filled with information on praise. As I understand the psalmist, he is saying that he will praise the Lord no matter what happens. He will constantly speak of His glories and grace. He will boast of God's kindness toward him. He then asks all who are discouraged to take heart and join with him in praise and exaltation of His name.

You can appropriate these words and speak them out right now. Imagine that we are sitting together or that we are in the midst of a whole congregation of people who are preparing their spirits to praise the Lord. Say with me:

"I will praise the Lord no matter what happens to me. I will constantly speak of His glories and His grace, for when I look at the Lord and look at His effect on my life and in the lives of His people, I see His goodness and His mercy."

One writer said, "I would have fainted unless I had believed to see the goodness of the Lord in the land of the living." It is so easy to look at the snow, the bad weather, and the rain that comes into your life. But when you look at God as your Father, you can praise Him. You can praise Him not for the things you have accumulated; not because He blessed you with a house; not because He blessed you with a car or with money; not because, through Him, you have received fame or fortune; but you can praise Him because He has blessed you with Himself, through His Son, Jesus. Because of God, you have the presence of Christ in you now.

You might ask, "How can I praise God in the midst of trial? How can I praise God when the fiery darts of satan come against me? How can I praise God when the clouds are hanging low and it is dark in my life? With all this to deal with, how can I praise God?"

You can't praise God on your own, because if you try to praise God on your own, you are too low in your spirit to praise Him. The praises must come forth from His Spirit working in you. The Holy Ghost within you will stir up the embers of His loving fire and bring forth the praises. You begin by meditating on God. When you meditate on His presence, the Holy Ghost takes over and lifts you to unknown heights beyond your human ability. Then you can praise God in spite of trials, in spite of tribulations, in spite of the things of life that are coming against you.

In Psalm 34:2 of The Living Bible, the psalmist tells us that he will boast of all God's kindness toward him. Those who are discouraged today: Take heart. You may have things happening that you don't like, circumstances you can't seem to change, or areas of your life that are out of control. Remember to take heart because the Lord is working things out for your good. Each event, by itself, may not seem to be good, but God is putting it all together and changing the bad to good. When you realize this simple fact of

God's action for good toward you, you can begin to praise the Lord and exalt His name.

In verse 3 we learn that when God's people come together to praise the Lord, the spirits of all the people are raised. Someone once said, "If I had 10,000 tongues to praise the Lord, I wouldn't have enough." I have an answer for him: "Just use the one you've got. It will work." Then, when you have three or four hundred folk together in one place, you have that many working tongues, all offering a sacrifice of praise to God. As they offer praises of adoration, exaltation, admiration, and worship, they will see the effect of each tongue as it works in unison with the Holy Ghost.

In verse 4, the psalmist goes on to say, "For I cried to Him and He answered me! He freed me from all my fears." Can you witness to the truth that you know the Lord has freed you from fear? He has freed you from the fear of what people will say; the fear of what the enemy tells you is about to happen; the fear of some disease the doctor is talking about. You are free from all the fears: the fear that you may lose your job this year; the fear that you may lose your home. Fears, fears, fears. In the midst of all this fear, God comes in and frees you from these fears because He "hath not given us the spirit of fear; but of power, and of love, and of a sound mind" (2 Tim. 1:7).

The enemy will keep you bound in your fears if you allow him. The thing that you fear the most will surely come upon you, if you don't know the key to overcoming fear (see Job 3:25). Listen to me, saints of God. When you feel a spirit of fear coming upon you, step out in faith and say, "Lord, I will not fear what man can do to me. I will not fear what others say about me. I will trust in the Lord until I die. I will not fear the things that may happen to me, for the Lord will answer me. He frees me from all fear."

In Psalm 34:5, it says that others too were radiant at what He did for them; they had no downcast look of rejection. And in verse 6, it says that this poor man cried and the Lord heard him and saved him. The Lord has saved you from a lot of trouble. If the Lord had not been on your side, what would have happened to you? Some people said you weren't going to make it and the enemy agreed with them. But in your spirit you knew the Lord heard your cry. One morning I awoke and began to call on the name of Jesus. Have you done that too? I called on Him and said, "Jesus, You know what the enemy is trying to do to me. I trust the battle to You." The victory is not for the Lord; the victory is for you. God shows His grace, God shows His love, through the victory He gives you in the battle. If you stand still and see the salvation of the Lord, He will fight your battle. Often we are too involved to stand still. We have too much of our mind and intellect involved. Make your mind be still and let the mind of Christ take over.

You have to get where you can rest in God and wait patiently for Him to produce victory in your life.

While you are waiting on God, though, what will He do for you? Isaiah said that God will renew your strength, and cause you to mount on wings as an eagle; He shall cause you to run and not be weary, to walk and not faint (see Is. 40:31). Cry out, "Lord, teach me to wait."

Then, in Psalm 34:7 we read that the angel of the Lord guards and rescues all who reverence Him. The angels of God are all around the saints of God because the angels encamp around those who fear the Lord. I am glad God has His angels camping around me. He gives them to us for protection. For this gift from God, I will praise the Lord at all times. I will praise Him in the morning, praise Him in the noon day, praise Him in the evening, and praise Him when the sun goes down. Along with all of God's creation that has breath to praise, I will praise the Lord.

Chapter 2

Let Your Praises Go Forth

Free to Praise

Today is the day the Lord has made and we choose to rejoice and be glad in it (see Ps. 118:24). I was attending an afternoon seminar and the person who was lecturing said something that made an impression on me. He said that until we understand and accept our creation by God, we cannot find our true identity, who we really are. If, for example, we believe that we evolved into what we are, we will miss who we really are. This speaker said that it takes more faith to believe we evolved because it's not truth. Evolution is not truth. We didn't suddenly evolve from some explosion, resulting in the random collision of atoms and so forth. God created us in His own image.

God created us in His own image and He gave us access to His creative power. He gave us power to have dominion, and the power of leadership. God's power is in us. His power is in us right now through the Holy Ghost. We really ought to be aware of who we are in Christ because Jesus brings us into perfect harmony with the Father. Now you have to understand that perfect harmony does not mean you are two people, God and you. You and the Father become one. So if you and the Father are one, you can't make two out of one. When you have one, you have perfect harmony. If you have two, you will have disharmony.

Why are we worrying so much? We worry because we look at ourselves as separate from God. Even some of you who are saved don't understand this concept. If you believe that you and your Father are one, you won't let circumstances damage your faith or shake you up. You know God is the only One who has everything under control and, since you are one with the Father, you have nothing to worry about, nothing to fear whatsoever. You have the power to step on satan. However, you're not stepping on him enough. You're letting him walk with you, talk with you, and entertain you. But you need to stop letting him talk to you. Don't let him hold a conversation with you. Don't give him your ear. Step on his head—crush him. Every time he sticks his head up, step on him in the spirit and in the name of Jesus. You will be victorious. You don't have to wait to get the victory; you have the victory now.

How do you know you have the victory now? Jesus said so. He said that He has overcome the world, and so have you (see Jn. 16:33). He is telling you that you are already victorious. You must walk with that attitude and with a victorious spirit. The walk with God is always spiritual. So you walk in the spirit.

In Psalm 51 there is a simple truth. It is about freedom in the spirit. In verse 12 we read, "...and uphold me with Thy free spirit" (KJV). Through God's Spirit, the Holy Ghost, I am free, and Jesus said, "Whom the Son sets free is free indeed" (see Jn. 8:36). I'm not in bondage anymore. I have a free spirit and that free spirit is God's Spirit. God created me to be free. He created you to be free—to be free from insecurity, free from dependence, free from worry, and free from despair. As a baby you had none of these insecurities. You were independent in terms of your spirit, and your physical body was completely independent from the time you were born.

As babies we are secure, but as we grow up, we learn all sorts of things. We learn to fear. We learn to be dependent on somebody to make us happy, to do this for us and do that for us. On the other hand, you can see children become more independent as they grow up. They reach a certain age where they don't want you to do anything for them. They don't even want you to feed them. Likewise, God has given you a freedom you should walk in so you don't have to depend on anyone to support you. Someone once told me he was trying to make somebody else happy, but no one can make anybody happy. You will be unhappy trying to make somebody else happy. The more you sacrifice yourself to make somebody happy, the more disappointed and the more frustrated you will become. God is the only One who brings happiness. When you realize who you are in God, you have happiness. You can share your happiness with others, but no one can make you happy. If you try to make someone happy, you will be disappointed in the end because the more you try, the more you're going to fail.

Now as you accept that statement as the truth about yourself and let go of the limiting thoughts that may have restricted your growth or kept you in bondage to certain conditions, you realize that no person has power over you. You are completely free to live your life. Nobody is to control you. No one has the right to dominate your life. No one has a right to dictate what you need to do with your life. You are the one who must take charge and recognize that God has given you the direction.

Is it correct to say that in all your ways, acknowledge your mother? Or in all ways to acknowledge your father? In all ways to acknowledge your husband? In all ways to acknowledge your wife? In all ways to acknowledge your friend? No! In all your ways you are to acknowledge God (see Prov. 3:6). Who is your director? You don't need two directors. If God tells you what to do, you don't need to listen to anyone else.

Does that mean you don't have to listen to the pastor anymore? First of all, you have to understand that God is speaking through the pastor. It's not the pastor; it's God in the pastor. When God speaks through a spokesman, you're supposed to hear God. You don't necessarily pay attention to the spokesman; rather, you listen for God in that spokesman. One thing is for sure, saints of God; when you hear God through that pastor and if you are listening through the Holy Ghost, there is a connection in your spirit that says, "Amen. So be it." You don't have to convince yourself because the Holy Ghost bears witness with your spirit and convinces you. Even if you fail to listen, or if you rebel on hearing His words, when you get home the Holy Ghost is going to tell you that you were wrong.

Before God lets a pastor lead his people astray for too long, the people will dismiss him or he'll retire. On one visit to Chicago, I heard of a pastor who was misleading the people and fighting against the doctrine of the Holy Ghost. It wasn't long before God took him out. God will remove the shepherd who does not feed his people. The Lord loves His sheep. He told Peter that if he loved Him, he would feed His lambs (see Jn. 21:15). He loves you so much He's going to have a shepherd who will feed you the living Word of God, and if that shepherd does not feed you, God will dismiss him and put somebody else in his place.

So when God speaks, that settles it. Do what God says instead of what other people say. We have a habit sometimes of trying to get everybody's approval. When God speaks to people, sometimes they walk around and talk to other people to get their approval. "What do you think about this?" When God speaks to me, I don't need your approval. You don't need approval when God speaks. God stamps His approval with His Word. He says to let every man be a liar, but let His word be true (see Rom. 3:4). I say that settles it. It may seem awkward to you, what I'm doing; it may seem strange to you, but He didn't tell you what He told me. You're free to live your life. Those people who live this principle live a happier, more peaceful life. They rest better when they go to bed, they work more effectively on the job, and they are easy to get along with. Yes, that's the truth. When you encounter someone who is mean, hateful, and hard to get along with, usually the problem is that they haven't found themselves in God. They have too many people dictating to them. That's why they live defensively. When you live your life completely, you are more at peace with yourself. When you are at peace with yourself, you can be at peace with other people.

Personally, I am free, praise God. I am free at this very moment in this very place. I do not have to wait for people to change or for conditions to be just right, for my freedom is assured right now. If the conditions are not to my liking, I am still free. Don't judge your freedom by your conditions, for conditions will lie to you.

The things that happen to our bodies are good examples of conditions that will lie to us. Some of you may have diseases in the body, but don't judge your faith by the body's condition. The body is feeble. It is something that will break down on you. Instead, let your faith be secured in your spirit and you will be strong. You may not be able to walk fast, but in your spirit you're walking upright. You're running and you're not getting weary. You're walking and you're not fainting. Your body may be slow, but your spirit is on the ball. The enemy can't hold you back because of your conditions. Some of you are looking at some messy conditions, but you are still free. The enemy does not have the victory because you lost your car or your house. He has no victory because the doctor gave you a bad report. He has no victory because you lost your job. He has no victory because your relationship is broken. He has no victory because something has happened with your children. You are free in spite of the conditions. The enemy can't cast your soul down. You're still rejoicing. You're still able to praise God because you know you are free, for the Son has set you free and you have a free spirit. Let the joy of the Lord manifest itself in your life.

The joy of the Lord is your strength (see Neh. 8:10). You are not strong because the conditions are just right, but because the joy of the Lord lives in you. When you would normally lie down and cry, the joy keeps you going. When you should be raising your hands in surrender to the conditions, the joy made you raise your hands to praise God. When you thought you should quit, the joy made you take another step. The joy of the Lord is your strength.

Also, you don't have to wait until you are in a certain place to be free. You're just as free on the job as you are in the sanctuary. Those who are in the prison ministry ought to take this message to the prisoners. Some of them have already found it out. You can be locked up behind bars, but if you are free in Christ, you're free. There are some folk who aren't behind bars, but they aren't free either. Don't worry about the conditions. You are still free in spite of the conditions. The enemy can't lock you up. He can't tie you up either.

When you are free and you know you are free, you ought to recognize that those around you are free also. Your loved ones are free to follow their own paths and to make their own decisions. Stop trying to make decisions for your loved ones. The worst thing you can do is try to make decisions for your loved ones. You love them so much and you say, "I want you to do this or I want you to do that." Leave them alone. Tell them that you acknowledge God in them and they are free to let Him direct their lives. If you tell them what to do, it may be the wrong thing and they will come back and blame you for giving them bad advice.

Sometimes people ask for your advice and when your advice turns out wrong, they hold it against you.

So, the best thing for you to do is to pray with them about their problem. You know that's the right way to handle problems. When you counsel people, you have no business trying to tell them what to do. Most of the time they won't listen to you anyway. All they want to do is get something off their chest, and what they are looking for is someone who will listen. They usually have their minds made up anyway. Whatever you say, they are going to do it their own way. You are simply wasting your time giving all that advice. The psychiatrist has them lie down and talk and they tell him what's bothering them. He says, "What's going on in your life? Tell me why you think that way. Has something happened to cause this? Do you think you ought to do something about it?" And these troubled people are answering all their own questions. All the psychologist does is hold their hands and help them make a decision. So don't try to advise people.

I found out something else. Folks who pass out a lot of advice usually pass out bad advice. If it was valuable, they wouldn't be passing it out for free. So let your loved ones be free to make their own decisions. Teach your children how to acknowledge God and let them ask God for direction. I know, as children, they need your help and guidance as they grow up. But as you teach them, they will learn to make their own decisions as they learn to acknowledge God. If you don't teach them and train them, what are they going to do when they leave your house? One day they will have to make their own decisions.

The first time my daughter, Sylvia, went to school, I was concerned. She is a young lady and you are always more concerned about the problems that face the girls. They are more tender and they are susceptible to a lot more things than men. Naturally the father wants to keep the girl home and let the boy go on. Sylvia was one who wanted to break away and talked and talked and talked until she talked her way out of the house and right into New Orleans. When she had an accident, she came back home and she went to Spelman College as a transfer student. I thanked God for her return, and then I decided to convince her that her original desire was to be at Spelman anyway. I wanted her to stay there, but she said, "Dad, I'm going back to school." I said, "What do you mean you are going back to school? I thought you were going to stay at Spelman." But she was determined to go back to school in New Orleans and I thought, "Here we go again." We had to reaffirm biblical principles in her so that when she returned to campus she would make decisions based upon her acknowledging God. We wanted to make sure that she was free in God to do all that she needed to do and to become all that God wanted her to be. We wanted her to grow to maturity and to be grateful for her freedom in Christ and express it every day.

Principles, God's principles, must be practiced on a daily basis in order for them to manifest. You can't take a principle one day, practice it that day alone, and then think that it will automatically work tomorrow. You must practice acknowledging these principles every day. This is a principle: You are free. You have to know you are free and you have to express it every day. When you wake up in the morning you ought to say, "I thank God for my freedom. I'm free, and I'm free to go in the strength of God. I'm free to make decisions. God is walking with me and God and I are one. We got this whole day together. This is the day the Lord has made, and I am going to rejoice."

You need to rejoice on a daily basis. You can't stay in the dust when you keep on rejoicing. You can't stay low when you keep on rejoicing. You should bless the Lord at all times and His praises should flow continually through your mouth. When you're free in the spirit, you can praise God more. When you know you're free, praises come out of you. It comes out of your innermost being. I see people who are all uptight, all stressed out. They haven't learned how to release the praise, for when you release the praise, it releases the tension. The more you praise God, the more the tension goes away. The more you praise God, the more you smile. The more you praise God, the more uplifted you feel. The more you praise God, the more you can deal with your conditions. The more you praise God, the more the doors start opening up for you. When you praise God, Heaven starts coming down.

Often, we are just not operating in the right way to get the effectiveness and the manifestation of deliverance. I told one woman, whose sister had been trying to commit suicide, to speak the Word. The Holy Ghost has revealed to me that you must speak to that demon of suicide saying, "I cast you out of my sister in the name of Jesus. I free you from that spirit. You shall not be tormented by it any more." When you speak in the power of God, demons will flee because He sent His Word to heal. He sent His Word to deliver. He sent His Word to set free. The word you speak is not your word. It is the Word of God coming out of you. It's in your mouth. Open your mouth and speak it. Speak to that abusive man in your house and set him free. He's not free; he's bound. He's bound by a demon of abusiveness. Speak to that demon, call it by name, and say, "I see you and, in the name of Jesus, you must go." That's the way you get rid of demons. You have to identify the demon. That's why demons don't want to tell you their names. But if you can get in the spirit, you can find out who they are. When you find out the name, call him by his name. Command it to come out of the person. Send it back to the pit of hell. At the same time, set that soul free in the name of Jesus.

You don't set the soul free by hollering, screaming, praying, and crying all night long or by complaining about your condition. All that noise and effort won't free anything because you haven't spoken the Word yet. You have not received because you ask in error (see Jas. 4:3). When you speak the Word and set the man free from that demon, do you know what happens? He changes overnight. I tell you the Holy Ghost can't lie. If you believe who you are, you know you have God in you; then, the Word of God is nigh, in your mouth (see Rom. 10:8). Use it. What do you think God gave it to you for? It's a sword. It cuts back and forth and the Bible says it will accomplish what it sets out to do. God says that His words shall not return to Him void, but they will accomplish what He sets out to do (see Is. 55:11). So when you speak God's Word, it will accomplish His purpose. You don't have to hope for it, so you can say it in confidence.

The Word comes out of me and I speak to that mountain. I'm free and I'm going to free everything around me in the name of Jesus. Go forth, saints, and use the Word He has given to you. Use the Word of God. Speak freedom. Speak prosperity. You run around pinching pennies and whining because you don't have any money. You don't have to be walking around here with no money when the earth belongs to God. He says, "For every beast of the forest is Mine, and the cattle upon a thousand hills" (Ps. 50:10 KJV) and "The silver is Mine, and the gold is Mine…" (Hag. 2:8 KJV).

But we must speak up and say, "I free my prosperity. I free my money. I have some money. I don't know where it is, but I have some out there in the universe somewhere. The money belongs to my Father, and my money, with my name on it, is out there in the universe. I speak God's Word to set that money free and come to me." If we put this thing together correctly, we are going to see some results. We are going to see some manifestations here. I don't have to wait on unemployment checks. I don't have to wait on social security compensation. There's money out there in the universe with our names on it, but we must speak to it and release it into our hands. Too many of us have our minds set on somebody giving us something. That's where we block our prosperity; we stopped at the resource and hadn't got to the source. We can't get it from the resource. The resource had to get it from the source in the first place.

Do you need oil? Maybe your resource is not giving you any oil. Go to where I got my oil from. Go to the source. When you go to the Source, you'll never be disappointed because He hasn't run out yet. God's oil wells are full and pumping. Until He stops the flow, you will always have something, if you know how to release it.

The system of man is always going to collapse. It will always go up and down. It's always going to disappoint you. But the system of God is consistent. You don't believe it? Wake up the man who testified that he used to be a young man and is now an old man, and has never seen God's people forsaken. His seed did not resort to begging (see Ps. 37:25). So, what are you begging for? Could it be you haven't found out how to work the principle? Speak freedom. You're on a job and you don't have to worry about them closing down shop. You confess there's a job with your name on it in the universe and you speak freedom for that job to come to you in the name of Jesus. The job will be yours because the Word will work.

For the dark places in your life, the Lord says, "Let there be light." To the dark corners in your life say, "Let there be light" and there will be light. God swore by His Word and whatever He says, He will do. He swears by Himself and He will do it. And if His Word is in your mouth, it's God speaking to the situation. He just needs you to cooperate. That's all He needs you to do. Open your mouth and speak. He can't make you talk. He can't make you speak His words. It's your decision to speak His Word. Then His voice will speak. He can take you to the fountain, but He can't make you drink. You're a free agent and you can make your own decision. Choose, this day, who you are going to serve. Are you going to serve your human flesh, your systems, your human governments, and your human economy? Then you will have to live by their principles and you will get the same results everybody else gets, even though you are saved by the Holy Ghost. But, if you walk after the heavenly systems that defy man's systems, you don't have to pay attention to the conditions or their appearance because they are illusions.

I speak in the light of Christ. I'll walk in His light and I'll speak in His light. And when I say, "Let light be," there's going to be light. I don't care what the system of government says. It will be light and they won't know how I got that job. They won't know how I got money when other folk are standing in the soup line. They won't know how I became the soup server. They won't know that I won't have to be a beggar, but I'll be a giver because the God in me owns everything. I'm never supposed to be on the end of the receiving. I'm always supposed to be on the end of the giving. And everything that I need to give out will come to me to give.

You have to walk in that freedom. To know is not enough. You must walk in it, practice it, exercise it, and use it. During one of our men's meetings, a member of our congregation shared an important principle. His mother was dying and had been given two hours to live. He walked in and said, "No, she doesn't have to die, because it isn't her time yet." His words stopped death and pushed it back out the door. He told death to go back where it came from and to leave his mother alone. She didn't die. She lived and she's coming back to testify. While others were saying she was dying and had only given her a few hours to live, this man was applying God's principle.

The other day some friends called their pastor to come to the hospital, saying that one of their relatives was dying. They started to prepare for her death, paying for the funeral and making all the funeral arrangements. He told them to call their relative's pastor, but they said it was too late to call her pastor. He insisted they call the pastor and let him speak to her himself. The same thing happened. She was supposed to be dead in two or three days, but after the pastor spoke words of life to her, she did not die. The principle works. I'm not writing something just to make you happy, even though it will make you happy when you start seeing the light. It makes you happy when it starts coming alive in you. But until you use this principle, it will be of no use to you. You have to acknowledge your position in Christ, act in it and walk in it, and that means to practice it.

Don't whine anymore. When there's a dark place, speak light. When there's something around you that is bound, free it up. Don't just free yourself. Set free those things around you. If there is confusion on your job, just try freeing it. When you find people who are confused, free them from their confusion. You speak it. Put the Word in your mouth, God's Word, and speak it and calm these people down. Free them from their frustration and misunderstanding of one another's personalities.

When I walk into a place, I want peace. I'm God's child. I deserve to have a peaceful atmosphere. I'm not going to let Heaven live in hell. Where I'm sitting is in heavenly places and I refuse to be subjected to hell in this atmosphere. So as long as I'm around here and as long as I work here, there's got to be peace in here. If you want to go back to hell's atmosphere after

I leave, that will be up to the others, but when I'm here, there won't be all this hell going on. I'm not going to endure all that profanity.

Now, I don't mean you have to go about correcting everyone or trying to straighten everyone out. I'm talking about your going to your spiritual laboratory and working it out in the spirit. I'll bind that spirit that is tormenting a brother or sister in the name of Jesus and free them from their profanity. Take that cursing spirit away from him so he can speak English. I'll guarantee you it will change the whole atmosphere. They will be wondering why it is so peaceful around you. You'll just be laughing and giggling to yourself. You don't have to tell them you've been practicing your freedom in Christ. The Lord Jesus didn't have to flaunt His power. Some of you want to flaunt your power. Don't flaunt your power; just use it. It's for your benefit as well as theirs.

Praise as a Holy Art

When praise is practiced as a holy art, we are rehearsing for the hereafter. Choirs must rehearse before they perform. Saints must rehearse for the main event—Heaven. Praise is the language of Heaven—the many acclamations of worshipful praise. You can study the Book of Revelation and find that the elect will be a people of praise forever more. A spirit of praise awaits us in our heavenly home. Why not prepare for it now?

We ought to praise God on earth because our joy in eternity will be to praise Him. No one can be ready for this eternal occupation if he does not practice now. We must praise God as well as petition Him. Petition is a superb form of praise. In asking God for anything, we are implicitly and explicitly expressing our faith in His ability to grant us that which we desire. We know, by faith, that with Him everything is possible, regardless of how miraculous the answer may be. We give God glory when we bring large petitions to the throne of grace.

God needs no itemized report of our requirements. His Son, Jesus, declared that our heavenly Father knows all that we need before we ask (see Mt. 6:8). But then there follows that word, that breathtaking promise, "Ask, and it shall be given you; seek, and ye shall find; knock, and it shall be opened unto you" (Mt. 7:7 KJV). Although our needs are well known to our Father, He still wants us to bring them to Him in prayer.

Is the prayer of petition the lowest form of prayer, as some people insist? If it were to be esteemed so lightly, Jesus would hardly have taught petitions by preaching and by example. A surprising number of petitions are woven in His priestly prayer in John 17. He petitions His Father, even though He knows His heart. God wants you to petition Him too. You can go boldly before the throne of His grace and ask Him. Nothing is too small, nothing is so large, that God will not listen to your request.

The plain truth is that our asking honors God because it demonstrates our belief in His power. It lets God know that we believe in Him as our Supplier. God is our source of all that we need. I go to Him in prayer. I don't have to back up from Him either. I go boldly, as I am instructed to do in Hebrews 4:16, and say, "Father, I stretch my hand out to You. I am calling on You and I need You to help me." Anything that you want to ask of God, you ought to ask Him now. When you start asking God and pleading with God and praising God, in the midst of that plea, Heaven will be shaken and the doors will swing open. The Lord loves His children and there is nothing too good for them. God wants the best for His children, just as you want the best for your children. Perhaps you try to give your children the best you can afford. Well, God loves you a million times more than you love your children.

You can stop reading right now and go to God. Why don't you say, "My divine Father, I give You praise, I give You glory, I adore You, I worship You, and I come to You with my heart open. Lord, feed me Your living Word and make ways for me, Lord. Open this door for me. Move the enemy off my track. Let demons be subdued. Give me strength in my hand, give me strength in my heart. Let my love be exhibited. Lord, let my light shine."

You must praise Him. You must petition Him. Sometimes the enemy will tell you not to say anything, but you've got to speak up. The Word says,

"You have not because you ask not. And, when you ask, you ask amiss" (see Jas. 4:2-3). You need to say, "Father, I'm going to call on You more. I'm going to be like the man crying out, 'Son of David, have mercy on me.' " They tried to shut him up, but he refused to be silent and he cried all the more. They told him to shut up because Jesus would not hear him (see Mk. 10:46-52). The enemy wants some of you to shut up, but you ought to open your mouth all the wider and cry out to the Father for mercy. Ask the Father to make a way for you. Ask the Father to open a door for you. Ask the Father to block the demons from your path. Ask the Father to heal your body.

We must get this clear—we must praise God. Let's praise Him, people. Let the saints rejoice. Let the saints praise Him. If you want God to answer you, you must start praising Him. If you've been talking to Him all day, spend some time praising Him. Whatever you've been crying out to Him for, start praising Him. "With God, the things you desire may not come when you want them, but they will come in time. I've heard your cries. I've heard your pleas. I've heard your groans, but don't stop praising Me." While you are waiting for a manifestation, keep on praising Him.

Chapter 3

Freedom for the Troubled Heart

There Is Hope

There is hope. Some of you may feel like there is no hope because all of a sudden you have been put out of your job. You may have even had the job for 15 or 20 years. You say, "What am I going to do now?" You must remember that the Lord says in His Word that the earth is the Lord's and the fullness thereof and the world and they that dwell therein (see Ps. 24:1).

So, if the Lord is the source, I don't look to the job to be my source. In the same way that God provided the resource, which was the job, He can provide another resource. Your hope as far as a job is concerned does not depend on AT&T or General Motors or any business. If your hope is in companies, you don't have much to go on because companies will fold.

Companies will go out of business. As Americans, we haven't seen anything yet. But when you have your hope in God and you understand that He will provide for you, then God will open a door for you. When your faith is released in God's Word, God backs His Word. God's promises are "yea and amen" and if God says He will provide for you, He will (see 2 Cor. 1:20).

Centuries ago, the Bible tells us, that God asked Abraham to go to Mount Moriah to offer a sacrifice. Isaac was to be the sacrifice. When Isaac, Abraham's son, couldn't see anything to sacrifice, he said, "Where is the sacrifice?" The Spirit of God in Abraham spoke out and said, "God will provide." (See Genesis 22.) That's the way God works. He puts His Word in your mouth and when you speak it, it comes to pass because God backs up every word He has ever spoken. He keeps every promise. There is hope.

Perhaps your father or husband or wife has left you and you don't know what to do. Well, I'm going to tell you something. God never told you to depend on anyone to give you love and happiness. God gave that to you when He gave Himself. He doesn't want you to put your trust in flesh because flesh may turn around on you any day. But if you put your trust in Him, and if that person is for you, He will bring him or her back. If that person is not for you, he or she needs to keep walking anyway. You must learn how to release those you love and let God handle the situations. You can't handle those things. You can't make people stay at home. You can't make folks love you. You can't make people like you. Only God can change the heart. There is hope.

You don't own anything that God doesn't want you to have. Some people say, "Well, you know, what the Lord has joined together, let no man put asunder." The Lord gave me an insight regarding that. He didn't join a lot of these people together before they started down the aisle. A lot of folks look at a person for all the wrong reasons. They choose their mates for all the wrong reasons. A woman may focus on this tall, handsome man that's got this big job and believe the Lord gave him to her. No, you're looking at his type. You're looking at his job and you're going to find out in a few years he wasn't the man you should have had. God may send you a little, short, dumpy man, but if God sent him to you, He can put some height on him in the spirit.

There are consequences to forcing a choice that does not line up with God's wishes. The crowded divorce courts demonstrate the results of those who were not joined by God. Why do I say that? God's Word reveals that people whom He joins together, no man can put asunder (see Mt. 19:6). If they go to the divorce court, they will remarry. But if God didn't join them together, they will break up no matter how long it takes, for God didn't put them together. So there is hope.

Some are crying, "Oh Lord, my children have gone bad on me." Don't you worry about it. There is hope.

If God gave you those children, God will save every one of them by your faith because He says you can sanctify your whole house by your faith (see 1 Cor. 7:14). The sanctified wife can sanctify the husband. The sanctified husband can sanctify the wife. He honors the words and the prayers of His saints and if you put those children in God's hands and say, "Lord, they're Your children and You will save them in due time and in due season," God will manifest salvation in their lives. He will do it. I know He will and I will tell you right now, He's going to do it. There's hope.

Don't worry that they're on drugs now. They're not going to be on them for long. Keep them before God and release them to Him. As long as you keep looking at the problem, you won't get a solution. As long as you keep talking about how your children are on drugs, they'll stay on drugs. Every time you say they are on drugs, you reinforce that power. When you start seeking God, saying, "God, they're Your children. I don't care if they have problems. You solve the problems. They have no sickness because You've already healed them. I'm holding them before You until it's manifested." Speak those things that are not as though they were (see Rom. 4:17). Eventually those children will lose their appetite for those things. They'll come in and say, "Mommy, Daddy, I was lost, but I'm found." If the Lord found you, He can find them. They are no worse than you were. Before God got hold of you, you were just as bad. You may not have been on drugs, but all sin, all unrighteousness, is in opposition to God's plan for your life. You may not have had some of these bad habits, but you were no better off than anybody else. So if the Lord saved you, He can save them. Leave them in the hands of God and keep speaking the Word. There is hope. Don't give up, for there's hope. It's not over until it's over. So believe God and you'll see what He's going to do for you. There is hope.

I face battles every day. I am facing a battle right now. The enemy in his own subtle way fights against those who are trying to walk the straight and narrow path. He's constantly got a war waged against you in the spirit world. He sends demons after you and they keep chasing you. They try to take you over. They try to take your mind. They try to cause all kinds of confusion in your life. But I want to tell you there is hope when you put your trust and confidence in Christ. Sometimes if you put your confidence in those you call friends, they'll turn around on you. They're not responsible. Demonic activity will take over your best friend and he will turn around and lift his heel against you. You must realize you can't put confidence in the flesh; you must put your confidence in Jesus Christ, the greatest Friend you could ever have. When you have a friend like Jesus, you can relax because He's the same yesterday, today, and forever (see Heb. 13:8). So walk with Christ. There's hope.

Let me tell you what hope does. Hope keeps you going when things don't look too good. Hope keeps you from worrying about those things in your life that you can do nothing about. Hope keeps you going when it looks dark everywhere. A preacher who visits our church occasionally, Dr. London, said one Sunday that everywhere he went in his house and every chair he sat in was engulfed in darkness, even though lights were all around. When he saw his wife suffering for five years at the point of death, he said it was dark. You cannot question God's sovereignty, but you can ask Him why (just as Job did). Don't question the situation; there is a purpose in everything that happens. Nothing can happen to you unless God lets it happen to you. If God lets it happen to you, you must keep your hope alive, saying, "Listen, I don't care what I see, there is hope."

Some of you are going through some storms right now. Some of you have already gone through some storms. The Lord woke me up this morning and when I looked out and saw the fog, I said, "I'm not worried about the weather in Atlanta. I want to hear about the weather of the saints." So I called Heaven's weather bureau and told them to give me the latest report. This is what they told me to tell you from Heaven's weather bureau: "Your storm is passing over. It may be dark right now, but the storm is passing over. Joy comes in the morning. There's hope."

I'm in the midst of a storm, but it's going to pass over. You'll walk through the valley, but listen to the Word, because you're not going to stay there. You're going through it and when you come out, you're going to look back over your shoulder and wonder how you made it through so many dangers, toils, and snares. I have already come through, but it was grace that brought this saint this far. Look up. Your day is coming. Look up, your King is reigning. Look up, your Father is watching over you. Look up, He's walking beside you, He's walking in you. He's going before you, making the crooked places straight. He told me to tell you, "I don't care how grim it looks—I want you to look beyond the clouds and see the sun shining."

The clouds are going to roll away one of these days. One of these days you're going to thank God for these experiences. You will realize that without sorrows you wouldn't know God could comfort you. If you didn't have burdens, you wouldn't know He could lift them. If you never saw the rain, you'd never appreciate the sunshine. If you've never been sick, you wouldn't know He could heal you. If you had never been unsaved, you wouldn't know that He could save you.

Through all my troubles, I've learned how to trust in Jesus; I've learned how to trust in God. I know there's hope. My hope is built on nothing less—not the economy, not the United States, not my money, not my friends, not my family—like the song *The Solid Rock* says, "My hope is built on nothing less than on Jesus' blood and righteousness" (written by Edward Mote and William B. Bradbury).

Let Not Your Heart Be Troubled

The Lord spoke to me one day and said, "If you wait too long, you miss your blessing." Too many of you are letting these troubling spirits distract you. You are allowing them to jump in your mind and trouble and confuse you. A saint is not supposed to be going through those changes. You are supposed to be helping others get out of their troubles. You attend church and you are praying, fasting, and living right. Still, you sit with troubled spirits and those in the world go on about their business. They are looking to you for some help and you are not prepared to help them because you don't know how to focus. You're not practicing the principles.

It's one thing to read Scripture; it's another thing to pull the principle out of it and put it into practice. People have come to our church and sat under our ministry for 20 years without seeing any change in their lives. They are only hearing the Word; they're not acting on it. You must begin to act on what you hear. You must work on your life. Some of you read books on how to be successful and how to make money and are as broke as Job's turkey. If you don't use the principles, what good does it do to read them? If you had the money you spent on the books, you'd be a millionaire. What's wrong with you? You get inspired and don't do anything.

Many people of color are good at that. We can get inspired and easily motivated, but don't carry it through. We get opportunities just like other people, but we're lazy. I'm not talking about any one individual; I'm speaking generally. We don't want to act. We want magic to happen. We want something to drop in our laps. God didn't put you on this earth for things to drop in your lap. You have to get up and do something.

My grandfather had a picture of this brother kneeling and praying. He told me, "If you want your prayers answered, get up off your knees and hustle." It is good to get down on your knees, but after you get off your knees, you've got to do something. You may ask the Lord to put food on your table, but He's not going to do that. God is not a waiter and He does not specialize in serving food to you. God will give you strength to get up and get yourself out of the house. He will give you strength to go to work and make some money to buy food. Then, you will be able to put food on the table.

You can sit there and pray, "Lord, send some bread by here," and you'll starve before your bread gets there. What the Lord's been showing me so vividly and wanted me to share with you is this: There are some things God isn't going to do—you have to do them. God works in the impossibility arena. That's the only place He works. He does not work in the possibility arena because that's where you work. God doesn't work in the human arena. He works where you can't work.

The secret is to learn how to rest in God. When you learn how to rest and do what the Scripture says, you allow God to manifest everything you need. The Bible tells us, "Let not your heart be troubled" (Jn. 14:1a). That's what Jesus is saying. There are too many troubled saints sitting around and shouting. Before they even get out of the Sunday service, they'll be going back down. It's like a slow leak in a tire. You go into a service station and you pump it up, but you know if you don't fix it, it's going to go back down again.

That's the way some of you are in ministry. You hear the pastor preach, you hear him teach, you get inspired, and you are ready to go on with the Lord. Before 24 hours pass, you are flat again and back in the same place you were before. The Lord wants you to get out of that troubled spirit. If you believe in the presence of Christ in you, you have no reason to be troubled.

There are some things that can catch you by surprise. They may daze you for a minute or two, but don't live in it. Break away from it and immediately go back to peace, back to experiencing the peace of God. Don't allow this troubled spirit to ride on your back. "Let not your heart be troubled" means not to live in the state of a troubled spirit. Don't live in that attitude and don't live in that atmosphere. Don't live in that mentality. A good way to support yourself is to stay away from those people who carry these troubled spirits. Stay away from those whiners, complainers, criticizers, and unforgiving people.

The Lord said something to me about forgiving today. He said, "Something my saints need to learn is how to forgive. They need to practice forgiving now more than ever because that unforgiving spirit is killing people." Unforgiveness is a slow cancer. I don't have to forgive you for your sake. I have to forgive you for my sake, for my health's sake. I don't have to wait for you to call me and ask me to apologize. As long as I hold on to that unforgiving spirit, I'm destroying my spirit. I'm destroying my mind and I'm retarding the spiritual forces in my life; they can't work with that kind of atmosphere. That's why the Lord Jesus said that if you won't forgive your brother, then the Father won't forgive you (see Mk. 11:26).

Some of you are sitting around with too much spiritual junk in you. That's what causes you to be troubled. A troubled spirit breeds off of junk. A troubled spirit breeds off of carnality. A troubled spirit breeds off of destructions. A troubled spirit breeds off of non-praise. You can rise above a troubling spirit through praise. If you feel troubled, shout: "Hallelujah, praise the Lord, thank You, Jesus." Shout, "I love You, Jesus." If you say it long enough, it will drop into your spirit and then that troubled spirit will have to go. Don't allow your heart to remain in a troubled state. If you believe in God—and I'm not talking about giving intellectual assent—

you will find that He is real. If you believe in Him, you are in tune with Him. If you believe in Him, believe in Jesus Christ whose presence is within you. I don't want you to live as troubled people. You are not supposed to be troubled people. You are not supposed to be miserable people.

Sometimes you might experience misery in the world and try to cover it up with pleasure. Underneath it all you really are not satisfied. You covered it up with fun, but you're not satisfied. You have had enough of that. When Jesus saves you, you may still experience problems, but your spirit, which is your consciousness, doesn't have to suffer from that troubled spirit. You can walk in the fire and not get burned. You can walk through the flood and not drown. You don't have to fear anyone or anything. Jesus did not give anyone power over you. All power is in God and all the power of God is in you.

So, what am I going to be troubled about? I want to share with you something which the Lord has dealt with me about. We give too much power and too much authority to things, people, and agencies. That is why, when you start learning there is no power other than God, certain things will not come upon you. There is nothing in this world that is greater than God. There is no devil in town that God cannot command. There is no demon that can overcome you because the power of God is over him. I speak and I walk in the name of Jesus without a troubled spirit because I have the power of God working through me. Are you worrying because the boss or the supervisor is trying to get rid of you? Don't give them that power. If you find out they're conniving and jiving, you say, "I rebuke these actions now in the name of Jesus. I have the power over you, satan, and I know what you're trying to do. You're not getting this job, for God gave it to me and I claim it in the name of Jesus. Any weapon formed against me is not going to prosper. Brother boss man, if you dig a ditch for me, you're going to fall in it. If you build a gallow, you're going to hang on it. I'm God's child, and I've got privileges. I'm a Privileged Christian."

Start walking like you know who you are. Walk in the Spirit of Christ, and you'll see how doors open for you. Before you get there, the door will be waiting for you to come through. That's why the devil wants to keep you all troubled. If you stay troubled, you can't build your faith and you won't be able to act on your faith. Without faith you can't please God (see Heb. 11:6). Without faith doors won't open, for you can't practice what you believe when you have a troubled spirit.

A troubled spirit keeps you vexed and angry. You start blaming folks for your failures and you start pointing fingers at them, saying, "If they hadn't done this to me, I would have been okay." I don't care what you think they are doing to you. Saints of God, stand up and say, "I don't care what people do because the door is already open. I may have some obstacles and I may have some hindrances, but I'm going to get there. And when I get there, I will show you better than I can tell you how the Lord created a problem to teach me how to use my faith. God puts obstacles in my way so I can learn from experience and, as I go through these obstacles, I learn how to be tried and tested and not be destroyed. I will not let this trouble me because God has a purpose for this."

Let not your heart be troubled. If you believe in God, believe also in Jesus Christ. Walk in the spirit of victory and the spirit of peace. I'm not worried, but some of Jesus' disciples were worried that He was going away. In a sense, Jesus really wasn't leaving them because He was sending the Comforter back. You're going to have more power now than you had when I was walking with you. Today I'm walking beside you, but when I go to the Father, I will walk in you."

I'd rather have Him in me than beside me because if He's in me, I'll never walk away from Him and He'll never walk away from me. I'll carry Him wherever I'll go. Do you know why He said, "I'm never going to leave you?" If He's inside you, He can't leave you. Also, you can't leave Him because you are joined together. You are one now and He will never leave you nor will He forsake you (see Heb. 13:5).

So, why are you troubled? Why are you crying, whining, and having a pity party when Jesus is living in you? God is with you wherever you go in any situation. What are you doing being troubled? "I just got a notice and they're going to evict me from my house," you complain. Wait just a minute. Are you letting that bother you? First of all, saints should not be so attached to material things. You have to learn to give them up.

The Kingdom you live in is not of this world. Romans 14:17 KJV reads, "For the kingdom of God is not meat and drink; but righteousness, and peace, and joy in the Holy Ghost." This means the Kingdom is spiritual. So what if you lose a house? So what if you lose a car? So what if you lose a job? What's the big deal? You are a spiritual creature and you don't need those things to survive. God knows what you have need of before you ask (see Mt. 6:8). Jesus told you to seek the Kingdom, so all you have to do is go seek the Kingdom and all the things will come back to you (see Mt. 6:33). Sometimes God lets you lose your possessions so He can get you into the Kingdom. Then He'll bring back better things than you've had before.

You don't believe it? Check Job out and see what Job did. He lost everything. Job said, "No big deal." He said, "The Lord gave, and the Lord hath taken away; blessed be the name of the Lord" (Job 1:21b). This doesn't sound like a troubled man to me. When you are troubled, you feel so bad you make up excuses to miss church. You think your problem has killed your spirit. If that's the case, you had the wrong spirit, for the Holy Ghost doesn't die. The spirit you were carrying needed to die.

You are a spiritual person and your residence is not even of this world. You are not a permanent resident of this place. If I'm rich in my soul, I can get anything I need for the body. That's why the Lord said, "Don't let your heart be troubled." Let your heart be at peace and full of love and walk in the strength of God and the peace of God. You can smile in your spirit when you don't have a troubled spirit. Eventually the smile will come out on your face. Don't be troubled. Don't be worried. Don't be vexed. Don't be discontented. Rest in the Lord; believe in Him. Trust and walk in His power. Walk in His strength. Walk in His wisdom. Walk in the spirit of peace.

When these words came to me from the Lord, I almost fell over. Then He told me to tell His people, "You must not let your heart be troubled." I replied, "Lord, why do You want me to tell the people that?" He answered, "Because there's too many of My folk with troubled spirits who are trying to glorify Me." Did you not know you can't glorify the Lord with a troubled spirit? That means you are not trusting God. You're not believing in Him. You can't praise Him and keep your mind on worldly things.

When you are praising God, you must control your mind. Don't let it wander all over the place. It can't be back home, worried about how you're going to pay those bills this week. You concentrate on the first of the month and all the bills coming due. It isn't the first yet. Besides, you may not even make it to the first. Did you eat today? Do you have clothes on your back? Do you have somewhere to sleep tonight? Why are you worrying about tomorrow? Who takes care of your faith? Is He going out of business tomorrow? What are you so troubled about? All of your troubles and all of your worries can end right now if you will simply allow Christ, who lives in you, to take control of your life. With Him in control, there are no troubled hearts.

Chapter 4

A Prophecy of Encouragement

I was on a radio talk show recently and a lady called and asked why good people have to suffer. She had lost a son who was 24 years old with his whole life ahead of him. She knew he had a lot to offer and she wanted to know why he had died. How many of you have asked, "Why?" There are those who say we shouldn't question God. I don't understand that kind of reasoning. If I can ask questions of my earthly father, why can't I ask questions of my heavenly Father? If anyone should know, it is God. That's why I'm asking Him. If anyone knows, God knows. He has the answer. I would rather go to Him for the answer than trust in someone who is going to give me his best guess.

God may not always give an immediate answer. Rarely, He may not answer at all, because the question is ridiculous and the answer should be obvious.

This sister who called the show while I was on had a legitimate reason for asking. Where can she go to find something that tells her why good people have to go through all these difficulties in a human world? Everything in the human experience is subject to change and is also subject to disharmony. Life includes suffering, disease, trials, and tribulations. Job puts it like this: Everyone is born unto trouble as sure as sparks fly upward. (See Job 5:7.) Now, where do sparks go? You know they go up, right? So, as sure as sparks go up, you can be sure that you are going to have some trouble. In this world you shall have trouble.

Why do we have trouble? It is because this world is full of sin. Wherever sin is, there is trouble. Why does your body suffer? It suffers because your body and the members of your body are full of sin. Paul said that in his flesh there's no good thing (see Rom. 7:18). That's why your body is in a deteriorating process. While it's healing itself, it is also deteriorating because of sin in its members. Deterioration comes as a result of sin—and the world we live in is full of sin.

So, there is going to be corruption, there is going to be trouble, there's going to be tragedies, and there's going to be all kinds of things that we don't like. But in the Kingdom, which is the spiritual dimension, there is no suffering, no sickness, no pain, and no death. The saints of God, looking forward to an eternal existence in a purely spiritual realm, are able to cope with the problems that confront them in the earthly realm. They understand and practice walking in the spirit and pay no attention to what's happening.

If you don't practice, you will not be able to cope with the things that are happening to you day in and day out. Without spiritual exercise you will spend your time crying, whining, fussing, raging, and going through changes, because that's what the world does when they don't know Jesus. When they don't have Christ, they start cursing and fussing and the least little thing frustrates them. They try to solve the problem by taking something to calm their nerves. But they won't find peace in a bottle or a pill. They are reaching out for all these substitutes, but they are still hungering inside. They will never be satisfied until they get the real thing, and the real thing is to allow Jesus to live inside them.

A saint may not have a car or a big home, but he has an unspeakable joy and he is full of the glory of God. The same things are happening to him. He's having tragedies; he's having heartbreaks; he's losing his job; he's having sickness in his body. All these things are happening to the saint, but he has Christ. That's what keeps him going. I know it keeps me going. If I didn't have God, I'd be doing a lot of things in an effort to keep my mind at peace. You must understand that if you don't trust God, you can't make it through all this trouble. I hate to inform you—you aren't getting out of trouble until you get off of this earth. All your heartbreaks and pains aren't over until you close your eyes permanently. Those who have gone over there will tell you, "I am not coming back. You can't invite me back. I'll invite you where I am because it's so much better over here that I wouldn't dare come back."

If you have ever been around a saint who is dying, you know he or she usually dies with a pleasant face because the person has seen something you are not able to see. It's like a peaceful night's sleep. When you wake up, you don't want to get up, do you? You roll over and try to recapture the feeling. That's the way it is in that new land.

Psalm 37 says never to envy the wicked, because they soon fade away like grass and disappear. Trust in the Lord instead; be kind and do good to others. Then you will live safely here in the land and prosper in safety. The fourth verse says to be delighted with the Lord and He will give you all your heart's desire. Isn't that wonderful? Don't tell me saints don't get what they desire when God says that all our needs shall be supplied according to His riches (see Phil. 4:19). I'm talking about saints. You may have to wait a little while, but you'll get it. If you delight yourself in the Lord, He'll give you the desires of your heart.

He gives you the desires of your heart because you're delighting in Him. When you delight yourself in Him, He can trust you with your desires. I tell you, you can get what you want if you delight yourself in

A Prophecy of Encouragement

God. Claim what you desire. Psalm 37 continues by telling you to commit everything you do to the Lord. Always commit the things you do to the Lord. One way to be sure you are committing things as you should is to seek God's approval before you make the decision. If it's a job opportunity, make sure God wants you on that particular job. Put your business in God's hands. Let Him be the chairman of your board. If you're establishing a relationship, let Him become a part of your relationship. In this way you will know if this is the man or if this is the woman for you. Commit it to the Lord. If it's a school you're planning to attend, make sure God agrees with you on it. When you commit it to the Lord, you will always make the right decision.

The sixth verse says that God will bring forth your righteousness as the light. This means your innocence will be clear to everyone. He will vindicate you with the blazing light of justice shining down as from the noonday sun. God has redeemed you, He has justified you, and He treats you just as though you've never sinned. And I'm so happy about that. God doesn't treat you as a sinner anymore. You're worthy now because God has made you worthy. You're a worthy child of God and, as His child, everything you get you deserve. As His child you deserve the best.

The reason a lot of us haven't gotten the best is that we didn't think we deserved the best. If you don't think you deserve the best, you won't get the best. You'll end up with second best. If you know you're God's child, you know God gives the best to His children, and you deserve the best. I'm not ashamed when I get the best God has to offer. I just stick my chest out and tell everyone that I deserve it.

You know what makes you and me deserving of God's best? We're God's children and God doesn't give His children secondhand stuff. We are first class citizens in a first class kingdom. We get the best and the other folk get the rest. God has made us the head and not the tail (see Deut. 28:13). We're leaders in the world, not followers. We show the world how to live a happy and fulfilled life and still be holy.

Psalm 37:7 tells us to rest in the Lord. That means to get in the Spirit and rest in the Lord. Give up some things. Set aside the troubles you're going through. Release your burdens and problems and put them in the hands of God. Don't spend time thinking about them. Put your mind on God. If it's something you can fix, fix it. If you can't fix it, put it over into the hands of God. When you give it to Him, He's the One who will fix it, so don't worry about it. As long as your mind is actively thinking about it, you haven't turned it over to God. As long as you're thinking about it, God can't work. If God allowed you to do the things that only He can do, you would end up wanting the credit. So rest in the Lord and wait patiently.

Waiting patiently is like waiting in a long line at the bank. You are often forced to be especially patient when the person in front of you is fumbling with his money or asking a whole lot of questions. The teller is doing her job, answering the questions and trying to complete the transaction, but all the while, ten people are held up. If you are like me, you have a hard time being patient under these conditions. I start moving and squirming and looking around. I'm waiting, but I am not very patient. In fact, you could say I am waiting anxiously.

I also get anxious when the car in front of me doesn't go when the light is green. In this crazy world we live in, I don't know whether I should blow my horn or not. Somebody may jump out and shoot me. So I look to see if the person in the car ahead is having trouble or something before I sound my horn. But I am not waiting patiently. Waiting patiently is when you're waiting without care, without anxiety. You are at peace when you're waiting and you're praying in the spirit as you wait. This is how you learn to wait patiently on Him. The more you trust Him, the more patiently you can wait. Soon you will realize that God has a reason for why He's not manifesting some things right now. He's got a purpose for that. He's got a purpose for having you wait. He's building your faith up in Him. He's building your trust in Him.

So I'm going to wait patiently, and while I wait I am going to offer praises to Him. God will act to do those things He's promised you, but you've got to wait patiently. Between the promise and the fulfillment is a period that's called patience. If you call me tomorrow from California and say, "Pastor Greer, I'm stranded out here and I don't have a way home. I don't have any money and there's no one to give me a loan." If the Lord moves on my heart to wire you money, you will have to wait. When I agree to help, you can't get upset and say you want it right now; it just doesn't work that way. I have to go to the bank and then I have to go to Western Union. Before I can send the money, I have to fill out the papers and wait for them to put it in the computer. Once I get to Western Union and the information is entered, the process may only take 15 minutes or so. But it took a lot of time to get to that point. And all the while you will have to wait patiently.

When I told you over the phone that I would send the money, you had a promise that was not yet fulfilled. Still, because you had the promise, you were willing to wait. God has promised us a lot of things too. But between the time He made the promise and the manifestation of that promise, you have to wait on Him. Meanwhile, you can begin to shout praises because if God promises it, you can count on receiving it. God said it and He can't lie. You may not have it yet, but it's as good as there. It's already done.

When a lady gets pregnant, it takes time before the baby is born. She can say, "I want this baby in two months and I'm not carrying this baby more than two months. It's too heavy and too many changes are going on." It makes no difference what she wants, the baby will not come until it's time and that time is usually nine months. Between the promise, the seed, and the birth, there's a waiting period.

What I'm trying to tell you is to get pregnant with the promise. Get pregnant with the promises God made for you and let patience possess your soul. Watch carefully, by and by He will help you birth the promise.

Verse 1 in Psalm 37 goes on to say that we shouldn't be envious of evil men who prosper. Stop your anger and jealousy and don't fret and worry. It only leads to hardness of heart and it will harm your mind and your body. The wicked shall be destroyed, but those who are the Lord's will be given every blessing. Wait patiently on the Lord.

Chapter 5

Getting the Best of Yesterday

There are a lot of things about your past that perhaps you don't like or that you would like to change. Still, you have to go on with your life because you can't live in the past. The Lord reminded me that you must forget the things that are behind you and go on with your life, pressing on toward the things that are ahead. If you really stand for the Lord, there are great things in store for you. Your best days are ahead if you're on the Lord's side, and if you walk in the center of His will.

Philippians 3:13 says, "No, dear brothers, I am still not all I should be but I am bringing all my energies to bear on this one thing: Forgetting the past and looking forward to what lies ahead." Paul is an excellent illustration of the man who got the best of yesterday. There was much that was dark and sinful in

Continual Praise

Paul's yesterdays. Much that, as a follower of Christ, he would like to forget and turn away from forever. In his yesterdays were his persecutions of the Church of Christ, as well as his blasphemies and his cruelties toward those who believed in Christ. But Paul conquered, forgot, left behind, and got the best of all that was dark, bitter, and sad in his past.

You may recall how he persecuted the saints in the name of God. Paul did these things in ignorance. There are some things you have done in the past that were bad, but you were ignorant. You didn't know any better. That's why it takes the light of Christ to show you the right way, to help you to see what is right and what is wrong. In Romans 8:28 Paul tells us that all things work together for good to them that love God, to the called according to His purpose. In retrospect we are all like the apostle Paul. We all have much that ought to be forgotten. It may be a word, a hurt, a transgression, or a sin, but through Jesus Christ, we have the liberty to forget those things that are behind us. We can do all things through Christ and one of the greatest things we can do is forget the things that are behind us. So forget the things that are past.

One of the greatest blessings of the Christian faith is the ability to forget the past. You have the power of Christ to help you overcome the past. You can't do it on your own. With human ability it is impossible to forget or not to dwell on the negative things in your past. But with Christ and in the power of the Holy Ghost, you can refuse to dwell on your past hurts and pains. God gives you the ability to overcome those things.

Are you a victim of yesterday? Sometimes I'm not sure which is man's greatest foe: yesterday or tomorrow. There are a great many people who are not willing to forget. However, in Christ all are able to forget the sorrows of yesterday. Sometimes what you do is permit your mind to turn back and focus on a sorrow or a loss until you are unfit for the duties of life. You become unhappy and discontented. You are not able to help anyone else when you live in the negative past.

Of course, there are good memories we can enjoy. To remember loved ones, who have departed this life, often brings comfort, guidance, or inspiration. It is only when we enter into self-pity, questioning why they were taken from us instead of focusing on the blessing they were to us, that we abuse the good memories of the past. We ought to think how wonderful it was to have had them in our lives and think of the good times we shared together. So don't dwell on the loss. Dwell on all you gained from their lives with you.

In that connection, the gratitude and resignation of Job, when he was afflicted, comes to mind. After he had lost his children and all his property, he said it was the Lord who gave and the Lord who had taken away. Still, he blessed the name of the Lord. (See Job 1:21.) Can you thank God for the things you have lost? We can always bless the Lord when things go our way, but when things are taken from us, can we still bless the Lord? I once heard someone say, "I will bless the Lord at all times, in my dark days as well as in my bright days. My praises are still going to come from my lips to say the Lord is a good God." A lot of things may happen that I don't like, but God is still a good God. As long as you have God, you haven't lost that much because God can make up for the difference. God can make up the deficit. God can make up for what you lost because my God will supply all of your need according to His riches in glory (see Phil. 4:19).

There are a great number of people who are the victims of painful and unpleasant experiences of the past. They are always turning back to some unhappy thing in their past. They are always talking about those who hurt them, those who wounded them, those who deceived them, and those who injured them. In some ways they are never able to get over it and that one event is like a slave driver to their souls. They are victims in a double sense. There was, first of all, the hurt of the wound or the injury. Then there is the constant resurrection of it by their unrestrained grief and their ever turning back to it. Not only have they not overcome the hurt, but they also keep resurrecting it every morning.

When you continue to think about how people hurt you, you're going to hurt more. You're going to give power to that hurt. It will never heal until you forget about it and get your mind on something else. You've got to learn how to occupy your mind with things that are good, things of good report, things that are pure. These are the things to focus your thoughts on. As long as you think of your hurt, you're going to hurt, hurt, hurt until you become paralyzed and can't go on with your life. So what, if your father took advantage of you as a child and abused you. So what, if your mother may have abused you. So what, if you do not have a mother or father. What can you do about it now? So what, if somebody molested you or raped you in the past. What can you do about it? It's done. It's over. The question is, "What are you doing with your life now?" Are you going to let it go down the drain because somebody abused you?

Jesus came to set us free and to bring healing to us. He came to bind up the broken heart and to bring salvation in our lives. Jesus wants us to learn how to place our past sins behind us—in the sea of forgetfulness and forgiveness—so that we will remember them no more. You must go on with your lives, my sisters and brothers. There are things that happened in my life that I don't like. There are people who have taken advantage of me. When you take it and turn it around and let God work with it, you'll come out stronger.

It is a part of the process of growth to be able to learn how to take the storms of life. You often begin as a child, grow into a teenager, and then, with all that experience behind you, you press forward to maturity. If you don't acknowledge your trials and deal with them in a positive way, you may become weaker. You don't go through the process. Stormy weather makes you appreciate the blue skies. With a silver lining waiting for you, you face the problem, take the challenge, and keep on pushing.

I'm so glad I wasn't raised in a rich family. There is nothing wrong with those of you who were raised in a rich family, but I stand by my own personal testimony. Had I been raised in a rich family, I might not appreciate how far I have come. I don't have to wear it on my head. I don't need to flaunt my successes, for I know where I came from. I had to struggle for what I have and for what I have achieved. As an adult I rode a bicycle because I didn't have a car. As a child, the best bicycle I got was secondhand, a hand-me-down from my uncle. I wanted an electric train, but I never got one.

My father and mother started preaching in a tent. They sacrificed, sold their house in Detroit, and moved to Chicago where they preached in a church. I lived in a barbecue hut while they slept in a tent and preached at a church. My brother and I had to sleep on one cot. He was down on one end and I was on the other. His toes were in my face and my toes were in his. Every night we would fight trying to get each other's foot out of our mouths.

The important thing to my father, in those days, was preaching on the street corner every Friday and Saturday and winning souls for Jesus. I may not agree with that method now, but at least he was doing what he knew best. He sacrificed for the sake of the ministry. Things that we, as children, would have liked to have enjoyed were not available because he sacrificed and gave everything back to the ministry. I always felt the ministry was wonderful, but you also have to feed your family. You need to make sure they get the best, if you're giving others your best.

Too often, when we look at people, we don't really know them or what they have been through. I lived with roaches and rats in that barbecue hut. Thank God, I don't have to live with the roaches and rats anymore. Still, I thank God for all that I have been through because those are the experiences that make me thankful. When you've been through difficult times and you overcome the difficulties, you ought to thank God, because He didn't have to put you where you are today. He didn't have to bless you like He has blessed you.

If He takes all my health, I still have Him. I can't worry about injury. I can't allow myself to dwell on it. I can't hold anything against the people who have hurt me because it will backfire on me. Hostility and hatred will kill your body, your mind, your spirit, and your career. We, as people of color, must get out of the spirit that sets us against the white man as well. We must put those pieces behind us and go ahead with our lives. You think you can't get a job because you are an African-American. Get your mind on God. God can make a way out of no way. Stop making excuses because you're Black. You don't need to make excuses, for the fact is you are somebody. You're God's child. You're some of the strongest people in the world. Why do you insist on giving up? Pick up the pieces and say, "I'm God's child and I can get what I want to get because God opens the door."

God can change the minds of those who are racists. You're hindering yourself by thinking of it. I know there's a problem, but it is the racist who has the problem. If you understand what I am saying, you won't have a problem and they won't be able to paralyze you. What about Booker T. Washington? What about the first man who invented the traffic light. They were Black Americans. The first open heart surgery was performed by a Black man. What about Jackie Robinson? What about Joe Lewis? Even if someone has a problem with my color, I'm still going to move on. I'm still going to do what I know I can do. I can do all things through Christ (see Phil. 4:13). Not through the system, but through Christ. Not through the government, but through Christ. I can override the government if I get in the Spirit. Who's over God? The United States government is not over God. Your employer is not over God. God is God all by Himself. He can move somebody and put you in his place.

I'm telling you to forget what you have been told. Stop talking about what they owe you. Nobody owes you anything. There is no Scripture to back up the idea that anybody owes you anything. If you go around with that attitude, you'll never get paid off. Why do you keep paralyzing yourself? May God help some of these children who grow up and think their parents owe them something. They don't owe you anything. They have taken care of you long enough. It is time you got out of that house and got a job. If you live at home, pay some rent. As long as you ride your parents, you will be a weakling in the world. You have to learn how to be a responsible adult. There comes a time when you have to break away. Even animals know that.

May God help you women who married some of these men who are irresponsible. If he doesn't take responsibility when he's young, he isn't going to take care of you. He will always be looking for a handout. When I got to be an adult, I didn't ask my daddy for a dime. If I had to struggle, I used those struggles to learn by. If I got behind in my bills, I learned to struggle my way out. When folks keep on helping you out, you'll never learn how to help yourself. That's why our homeless shelter at the Cathedral doesn't just house men. We want to show these men how to get back on their feet so they can help themselves. If you just keep on feeding people and don't teach them how to feed themselves, they'll always be asking for food. The same God who takes care of me and takes care of you can take of others, but they have to be aware that your God is their God too.

Why do you have to shout so loud? It's because the Bible says, "Cry aloud" (see Is. 58:1). You can recognize thunder by its sound. That's what the Lord is calling me to do through this book. He wants me to "cry aloud." He wants me to lift up my voice like a trumpet and show His people their transgressions in the house of Jacob.

So, forget those injuries, forget those hurts, forget what someone may have done to hinder you and move on with your life. You have got to forget your hurts. You've got to forget your insecurities. You've got to forget those who have deceived you. You've got to forget those times when you have had to face the darkness; move on with your life in Christ. All of us have had enough in the way of sorrow, hurt, wounds, injury, or disappointments, which, if constantly dwelt upon, would poison our spirits and disqualify us for the work of the life that Christ has given. Paul says that the one thing he wants to do is forget the past (see Phil. 3:13).

I'm not where I want to be at this point. Are you where you want to be? If you can answer "yes" to that question, you are ready for the grave. You have nothing else to learn, for if you have arrived at the end, you don't need to stay in school anymore. Don't sit in the class if you have already graduated. Why repeat the course when you have passed? So, if you have arrived, you don't need to read any further. You know everything you need to know, so there's nothing else left to learn.

When you have arrived, you can say you have finished your course. If you are honest, however, you will admit that you don't know everything and that you are far from finishing the course. If you are honest, you will admit you haven't reached the end, but you're pressing toward the mark. That is why God gives me a message to write. He wants to teach you more about this life. He wants to teach you how to deal with life's problems. He doesn't want you to sit and be paralyzed by your past. There is much too much to be done for the Lord, so you have to pick up the pieces and go ahead.

You know if every one of you would testify about some of the things that happened to you in the past, it would shock some of the people sitting around you. Some people take the attitude that they are going on with their lives while others sit up and meditate on their negative past, day in and day out. Ultimately, they become paranoid. They think everybody is out to get them or to hurt them. They can't relax anymore. They can't trust anybody when in reality, there are many people who do love them.

There is somebody praying for you right now; some don't even know your name. They are God's prayer warriors; they are in tune with Him and they love God's people. This should be music to your ears. This should change your thinking and give you a new attitude toward life. When you get a good attitude about yourself, you don't have to worry about those who have bad attitudes. They usually don't come around you much. When you have a smile in your spirit, you attract smiling spirits. Every once in a while you run across somebody who insists on being a grouch, but most of the folk you attract will be like you. Look at the folk who come to your church, for example. If they are like the people in my church, most of them have good attitudes. I have members come up to me and say, "Pastor, this is the friendliest church I have been in. The people are all so friendly and nice and always speaking to me." Then I'll have one who will come right on the heels of such a person and say, "These people are so stupid and nasty and some of them don't even know how to speak to people." I'll watch them because if they have a bad attitude, that's the kind of people who come around them. The result is they think the whole church is like that.

Even with everyday experiences, if you have a good attitude, then when you go to the marketplace or go on your job, you usually attract people who are kind. When you run into someone who is unkind, it is a shock, for you are so used to nothing but kind people. If you are to have friends, you must reach out to people. If you want love, give some love. What you give will be multiplied back to you. That's the principle in the Bible. If you send it out, it comes back to you. What you sow, you reap (see Gal. 6:7).

God gives you the ability to forget. This is not done on a human level because no human being forgets hurts and injury. They dwell on it. They live in the past and the present. They try to combine the two. But it won't work well that way. They can't be as effective as they would be if they could get out of that. But Jesus heals your inner man. It's an ongoing process. Whenever something else happens, He heals that. And He continues to heal, heal, heal because He wants you well in your inner man, which is the place you live out of. You don't live out of the external body. You live out of the internal, the consciousness inside the soul. Nobody can make you happy because happiness comes from within. If you have happiness within, you can share that happiness. And if you have happiness within, you don't have to have a Cadillac to be happy. You can use your footmobile. Walk until the Lord blesses you with a car.

Meanwhile, don't be intimidated because you don't have things. As long as you have peace, as long as you have happiness within, you can sing in the night season. You can sing if you have nothing but a tent. When you learn how to praise God in spite of what's going on in your life, He can start showering you with blessings. He gets turned on to people who suffer and still praise Him. He gets turned on to saints who may be wounded, but who are praising His name as they wait on Jesus to heal them.

You've got to know how to deal with stress or you will become distressed. You end up getting wrinkles before you're supposed to have them. The best thing in the world is to forget those negative things because they're hurting you as long as they dwell in the mind. The mind controls the body and the body will respond with disease.

The Lord chastises us and corrects us once we are in Him. He corrects us because we are His children (see Prov. 3:12). Just as you correct your children, God will correct you. He's not going to let you get by without correcting you. Don't tell me God can't change you. He transforms you. You know what you used to be like without God and you know what you are like now. You have come a long way. If you haven't come a long way, you aren't in Christ, for if any man be in Christ, he is a new creature. Old things pass away and all things become new (see 2 Cor. 5:17).

Recently, after a church service, someone was complaining about a couple of children, a brother and sister, who were disruptive. One of the ministers said to those who were reporting the kids, "Listen. Just thank God they're saved, because if they weren't saved, they would be meaner." This illustrates my point, which is this: No one has arrived or become what he will be. Just look at where you have been and who brought you to where you are now. Thank God, I am not what I used to be. You wouldn't want to see me as I used to be. I've come a long way because I've learned to forget the past. You've got to learn how to forget the past too.

The past will flash back to you once in a while. But you don't have to entertain the past in your mind. It may knock on your door, but you don't have to let it in. Put your mind on something else. When you walk up to that brother or sister who said something really nasty to you, that comment will often flash back. You have to catch yourself and pray for the Lord to sustain you. Ask Him to keep you in the hollow of His hand, in the center of His will. The best way to maintain a forgiving attitude is to sustain yourself in Christ. When you learn how to practice your life in Christ, you will be able to go through some hard problems.

What do I mean when I say, "Getting the best of yesterday"? What I'm referring to in this chapter is learning how to use past experiences as a springboard for moving on with your life. Life is not always easy and the Lord did not promise us a bed of roses. Into each life some rain must fall. But, if you learn how to trust God and know that through Christ you can take it, through Christ you can make it, then you can say like Saint Paul, "No, dear brothers, I am still not all I should be but I am bringing all my energies to bear on this one thing: Forgetting the past and looking forward to what lies ahead" (Phil. 3:13). That means you are concentrating on one thing, forgetting the past. But I'm not just going to forget the past. I'm also going to look forward to what lies ahead. I am going to trust the Lord to work all things together for my good, for I am one of "the" called of the Lord and I am called according to His purpose (see Rom. 8:28).

Paul was training to reach the end of the race and to see the prize which God had for him. God was calling him up to Heaven because of what Christ Jesus has done for him. Jesus is our hope for what lies ahead and He is our example for success. We can start shouting now before we see the manifestation. When they thought they had Him down, when they crucified Him on the cross and laid Him in the tomb and thought they had gotten rid of Him, He showed them all. On the third day God raised Him from the dead. As for us, Paul said that this same Spirit, who raised Jesus from the dead, will quicken our mortal bodies (see Rom. 8:11).

Chapter 6

Standing Firm in Praise

Be Strong in the Lord

Often events take place or things happen that you would have never dreamed could happen to you. This has happened to me. I believe it is a test of our faith when the unexpected comes. The Lord reminds us that, just because we are believers in Christ, we are not exempt from the trials and tribulations that are in this human arena. The trials of life are not always pleasant and if you don't have faith and confidence in God, they will devastate you. That's why we should stick together, love one another, and support one another in prayer, for all of us are struggling together. There should be no need for jealousy, envy, and strife between us. We should not rejoice if a brother or sister errs and falls. We should pick that person up and encourage him or her to go ahead because all of us have things hidden in the closet, and we would rather not open the door.

Don't pretend you have it all together when you know there are things you don't want exposed. Don't rejoice when you see others fall. Put your arms around them, pick them up, and say, "Go ahead, you can make it," because you may fall tomorrow. You don't know what you will face tomorrow. You are where you are by the grace of God. You must learn that your only hope is in Christ Jesus. "You dare not trust the sweetest frame, but you wholly lean on His holy name" (*The Solid Rock*, written by Edward Mote and William R. Bradbury). Stand on the solid rock of Christ. Otherwise life will do you in. We all must experience momentary light afflictions, but God gives us grace to keep going.

> *This book of the law shall not depart out of thy mouth; but thou shalt meditate therein day and night, that thou mayest observe to do according to all that is written therein: for then thou shalt make thy way prosperous, and then thou shalt have good success. Have not I commanded thee? Be strong and of a good courage; be not afraid, neither be thou dismayed: for the Lord thy God is with thee whithersoever thou goest* (Joshua 1:8-9 KJV).

God has commanded you to be strong, to be of good courage, and to not be afraid. There are some things we are exposed to that we never thought would happen, things that catch us by surprise. And the only way that we are able to go through those periods in our lives is to focus on Christ and know that God is our source and our strength. He is a very present help. He is not out there somewhere in the sky. He's not over yonder. He's a very present help inside of us and He is able to sustain us in spite of present circumstances.

Joshua in the Hebrew means "Jehovah will deliver." Jesus means, "Jehovah's salvation." Jehovah is the God of deliverance and salvation. God, the source of salvation, saved or delivered us through Jesus in the same way He saved the nation of Israel through Joshua. In this day and time in your life He's the source of your deliverance. He's the source of your strength and He is your joy. You have no joy outside of God. The world offers passing pleasure or tempts you with temporary happiness, but God is eternal joy.

The joy of the Lord is your strength (see Neh. 8:10). He told Joshua to take these people across the Jordan and into the Promised Land. They were more prepared to cross the Jordan under the leadership of Joshua than under the leadership of Moses. Under the leadership of Moses the people were confused. They had wandered many years and had lost a whole lot of time. But during their time in the wilderness, the people learned discipline through faith. If you wander in the wilderness long enough, you learn how to walk and move by faith. Their experience prepared them to cross over into Canaan, the Promised Land, to receive and reap the benefits that God had in store for them.

In Joshua 1:8 God tells Joshua that the book of the law shall not depart out of his mouth. He goes on to tell him to meditate therein day and night. He wants you to take His law and meditate on it day and night. He wants you to meditate on it so it will get it in your spirit when you speak. When you meditate on God's law, it gets in your spirit and you will speak His law and live by His law, and you will overcome. What He wants you to do is to meditate day and night and to observe to do according to all that is written therein. You don't make your own laws. You don't do whatever you want to do. You are not led by human thinking or your mind. He wants you to follow His instructions without wavering.

Often you suffer because you depart from the law of God. You try to do what your mind leads you to do and your mind will lead you into a hole. It will lead you to destruction. It will lead you into a trap. That's why you have to meditate on God's law and get His law in you where you can speak and act on it. What do you meditate on day and night? Television? Some of you watch television day and night. That is one thing you are faithful to do. When you're at home and not working, you're going to catch some program. You'll find out that "all your children" don't belong to you. You're going to find your "general hospital" is full of sex and lies. You will look for "the guiding light" when the Light that guides lives in you. You can really turn that light on by meditating on God's law. God's principles, working in you, will change you for the better.

The rest of verse 8 in Joshua 1 is important too. It completes the principle and causes the knowledge you have gained to work for you according to God's purposes. The second part of the verse tells you to observe all that is written within the law of God. What good is knowledge that goes unused? If you know how to fix a car, but don't use this knowledge when your car breaks down, you will be walking. You must use the knowledge. Once you use the knowledge and make the repairs, you will be riding once again.

There is a reward for the proper use of knowledge. The last part of this verse outlines the reward for doing what God is asking. The third part promises to the person who meditates day and night, and then observes or acts on the law learned during meditation, a prosperous way and good success. That is what we are all trying to achieve: God's prosperity and good success in our lives.

It's all right to go to school and educate yourself. Education is a good goal. But you will be more successful with your education if you first observe the principles written in this verse. More importantly, you will have success and prosperity all the rest of your life. God didn't put you on this earth to be a failure. God put you on this earth to be successful, to succeed in your endeavors according to His will. Nobody is supposed to flunk out. We flunk out because we won't practice what His Word says. Without God, you cannot be successful. You may build a material empire, but a man-made empire produces a hollow success. True success comes when you discover what God wants you to do and you obey Him by fulfilling His purpose. That's what success is all about.

America has mixed up people's minds by offering the wrong formula for success. Success is not a big car, a mansion, and a lot of money. Often those who have acquired such wealth are broken inside, confused, and without peace. You don't need to be running around not knowing what you are doing and what's going on in your life. That's not success. When God created you, He had an assignment for you. If you concentrate and meditate on God's Word, you will discover what you need to do. Once you begin to do what God wants you to do, you will be successful and you will prosper.

People who are successful in God prosper automatically. Prosperity will come to you because you are doing God's will. If you take care of God's business, He will take care of your business. The material things of the world are yours to use. He wants you to have houses, land, appliances, and cars. But He wants you to be successful in His ways first. He doesn't want to prosper a flunk-out. He doesn't want to bring prosperity to you while your life is a shambles. He wants you to put first things first.

Jesus said, put the Kingdom first then the other things would be added (see Mt. 6:33). Don't get the order backwards. God's order is always clear. He wants you to be prosperous and healthy instead of lacking in your finances and sick. He wants you to prosper in all areas of your life. He is not a God who accepts an incomplete effort. He wants you to be complete and perfect in Him, and then He wants to give you the whole thing. God wants you to smack your spiritual lips as you taste and see that the Lord is good. Every day you ought to take time to taste God's presence. You ought to wake up and smack your lips and say, "God, You're so good. I'm eating Your Word daily." When you get wrapped up in His Word like that, you're successful and you'll attract prosperity.

Doors will open that you think can't open. By the time you get there, they will open for you. When you walk down the street, He'll go before you. He will make the crooked place straight, raise the valleys, and lower the mountains (see Is. 40:4). He promised to open the windows of Heaven and pour out a blessing so large you won't have room enough to put it away (see Mal. 3:10). Complete prosperity comes to those who are in His will and if you follow His instructions and do what He tells you to do, you will have strength, success, and prosperity.

Finally, Joshua 1:9 KJV says, "Have not I commanded thee? Be strong and of a good courage; be not afraid, neither be thou dismayed: for the Lord thy God is with thee whithersoever thou goest." This is the central theme of this passage. He has you successful and prosperous, but He commands you to be courageous. He wants you to be spiritually daring, to go forth knowing that He will be beside you and that His strength will be your strength. I'm telling you, if you have God's strength, nothing will overcome you. With God's strength you stand before great men and women and boldly say, "I'm a child of God. I'm the King's child. I'm strong in the Lord. I know in whom I have believed. He is able to keep me from falling and flunking out of this life. Whatever I'm facing, I am strong and of good courage because I lean on God."

As a pastor and preacher, I am often tempted to hide in a corner and have a pity party. It often seems like things are falling apart around me and I want to run. I ask the Lord, "Lord, why would You let this happen to me when You know I'm doing Your work? I am taking care of Your people." He said, "You are not such a big deal. You're doing what you're supposed to do. Don't be throwing your record up to Me." Too often we try to bargain with the Lord by listing our accomplishments. We talk about the way we live such a good life, not like others who do what they please. When you start thinking this way, remember that God said not to fret yourself because of evildoers who prosper in their ways; they will soon be cut down as the grass on the earth (see Ps. 37:1-2). Those who trust in Him will live a Godly life in Christ and will suffer persecution.

When these words came into my mind, I wanted to whine some more, but the Holy Ghost in me said, "Shut up and praise God." You must praise God in spite of what's happening to you. Find a reason to praise Him and if you can't find a reason, praise Him just for being God. If He doesn't do another thing for you, He's done more than enough. Cut out the pity party and admit that God is able. Cry as the other saints have cried, "If You don't bring us out of the fiery furnace, You're still able. If You don't bring me out of the lion's den, You're still able. If I don't get out of this, You're still able. In the meantime, while I'm in the fiery furnace, while I'm in the lion's den, while I'm facing all these problems, I'm going to praise You. I'm not going to let it keep me down."

Don't let anything keep you down. It may stun you for a minute or two, but brace yourself and be strong and of good courage. You can make it. The Lord told me that anything that doesn't kill you makes you stronger. It may almost kill you, but if it doesn't, it will make you stronger. Conflict brings the best out of you. I don't understand it, but it happens. Whatever you've been through has made you stronger. It will either make you stronger or make you bitter. Bitterness never changes anything, so you might as well be happy in the midst of your circumstances. It's much better to stop kicking, crying, and screaming. It's better to be calm while everything is happening. It makes no sense to run your blood pressure up because, when you get through running it up, the problem remains. So, you might as well calm down in the storm. Just rest in the Lord and wait patiently for Him. God won't allow more to come upon you than you can bear (see 1 Cor. 10:13).

The problem is we simply don't want to have anything happen that is against our own will. We never consider the opportunity that may come through adversity. The Lord knows His children and He knows what they can endure. You wouldn't tell a child to pick up a 50-pound load. That is a job for an adult. That's the way the Lord treats you. He doesn't put any more on you than you have the strength to carry, for He doesn't want you overloaded. He just wants you to take responsibility for the load to develop you and to make you stronger. Then, when you get through with that one, He will give you a heavier one so you can get even stronger. His whole purpose is to help you become more effective in His hands.

The job that we do and the life that we live is to be carried out without fear. We are not to be anxious or afraid. What are you afraid of when God is with you? I will not fear what man can do unto me (see Ps. 118:6). The Lord is my light and my salvation, whom shall I fear? (See Psalm 27:1.) I don't fear man or woman. Man can do nothing to me unless God lets

Standing Firm in Praise

him. I'm in His hands, in His care, and I'm working to fulfill His plan.

In Acts 7 we read the story of Stephen. God allowed him to be stoned, but it was for a purpose. He wasn't mugged or robbed. He was stoned to death for a purpose. Stephen knew the stones wouldn't kill him. He knew he would live on with God in Heaven. Before his body failed, he looked up and saw Jesus standing on the right hand of the Father. The real Stephen didn't die, only the shell we call the body. They couldn't keep him down there in that hole. He was not afraid. Don't be afraid, just deal with it the best that you know how. Let God lead you and fear will not overtake you. Don't let fear shake you. If you lose your job, don't be afraid, don't panic. God is your source. He gave you that one and He will give you another. Most of the time the second job is better than the first.

Whatever you are going through, you can make it. If I can make it, you can make it. As I look back on my own experiences, I see the hand of God leading, guiding, and directing me. He brought me through and He will bring you through. You may say, "But you are a pastor." You must understand, God is not a respecter of any particular person (see Acts 10:34). We are all alike, regardless of what we do.

Do you know why you don't need to be afraid? Do you know why you can be strong and of good courage? Do you know why you don't have to be dismayed? It is because the Lord your God is your Master, your Instructor, your Director, your Conductor. You have the Chief Architect of the universe as your partner in life. The Lord your God is with you wherever you go. If you go to the mountain, He's there. If you go down to the valley, He's there. If you go across town, He's there. If you go on the job, He's there. If you go home, He's there. Wherever you go, God is with you. That's why you can be strong. That's why you can have good courage. That's why you don't have to be dismayed. That's why you don't have to be afraid—because the Lord your God is with you wherever you go and if He's there, He's got everything under control. You will prosper. You will succeed. You will enjoy good success in spite of what's going on in the world.

Don't put your hope in the economy. It's already messed up. The country's already broke. Don't base your hope on your good job. Base it on the Lord who is with you wherever you go. He won't let you down. I read something and the Lord spoke through what I was reading. I read that the saints can survive a depression if they are conscious of Him. He is the One who provides for the saints. One of the saints from the past said, "Once, I was young and now that I'm an old man, I have never seen the righteous forsaken nor his seed begging bread" (see Ps. 37:25). Whatever happens in the world, in politics, in the economy, or wherever else, the saints will not be forsaken. As a saint of God, I depend on Him to be my source and my strength. The Lord is my shepherd and I shall not want.

Chapter 7

Stand Firm in Faith

Trust in the Lord

Isaiah 12:2 KJV says, "Behold, God is my salvation; I will trust, and not be afraid: for the Lord JEHOVAH is my strength and my song; He also is become my salvation." Place your trust in God and you will be strong and assured. Some situation, person, or event may prompt you to feel anxious. There are certain things that cause you to worry and, momentarily, you feel anxious. That's why you have to learn to trust God completely in those situations.

Suppose you lost a loved one, a child or someone in your family, suddenly through a tragic accident. Suppose you went to your job some morning and they told you that your position was eliminated. Suppose you woke up to find that you had a broken relationship. Suppose your child had been put in jail. Suppose you found out that you have a terminal disease. What would you do? The only way you could survive is to put your total trust in God. If you don't trust God, you can't make it through unexpected problems.

There are many people who can't take it because they don't know how to put their trust in God. Regardless of how long you have been saved, there are times when you feel like there is no hope. There's a time when you feel defeated. There's a time when you have doubt in your heart. It is at those very times that you need to pray, "Lord, help my unbelief and increase my faith in spite of what I am facing. Lord, help my unbelief."

When the disciples were on the ship with Jesus, a storm came up. They began to get anxious and they tried to wake the Master. They thought He didn't care if they all perished in the sea. They didn't know that, as long as Jesus was in the boat, they need not have feared the wind and the sea. They didn't know that He was protecting them. Jesus was not anxious because He trusted the Father. He had to calm their fears and take away their anxiety. They had lost their focus and Jesus helped them regain it, as well as faith and trust in God. He spoke to them and said, "Listen, you don't have to worry about this storm. I'm in charge here." He spoke to the storm and said, "Peace, be still." (See Mark 4:35-41.)

There is no crisis in your life that God can't sustain you in if you fully trust Him. You have to learn that nothing is greater than the One who lives in you. No circumstance, no problem, no event, no person, nothing outside, nothing above or below, is any greater than the power that is in you. "Greater is He that is in you, than he that is in the world" (1 John 4:4b KJV) and there's nothing that can come upon you that God can't keep you safe from. You must trust Him in your dark days as well as in your bright days. You will go through some dark times. You will go through some lean times. You will go through some valleys. David was able to walk through the valley of the shadow of death and not fear evil. He knew the Lord was with him. I will not fear what man can do to me because God is my help.

I can trust God now more than ever before because He has established a track record with me. Can you look back and see the things He's brought you through? Can you see some things He's helped you to go through when you know you could have collapsed? Have you seen Him act on your behalf? If God has blessed you from that time up to this time, He can take you on to the end. This hymn of praise says, "Behold, God is my salvation." Who is my salvation? God! The salvation God offers includes safety and preservation. He continues to deliver you out of situations. Salvation is a one-time event, but the process is continuous.

Before the three Hebrew boys were put in the furnace, they made something clear to those who put them in there. They said, "If we don't come out of here, we know He is able." (See Daniel 3:17-18.) You must learn that if you don't come out, God is still able. That's trusting Him. If I don't get healed, He's still able. When they went into that furnace, they kept walking around. They were not bothered by the heat. Not even their hair was singed. The people outside could see the flames and they could see the figures walking in the midst of the flames. They expected to see them burned to a crisp. Instead they saw not three, but four figures. And the fourth looked like the Son of God (see Dan. 3). Isn't that just like Jesus? Wherever you go, even if it's a fiery furnace, He's still with you. If you go through the fire with Jesus, you won't get burned. If you go through the flood with Jesus, you won't drown.

Life is full of problems. Life is full of ups and downs. Life is full of changes. Man is born as a troubleshooter. The sparks fly upward, but when you learn to trust God, you can rest in the midst of the storm. It's just like the little bird I saw in a painting. He's nestled in the crevice of a rock and the rock is overlooking the sea. The sea is all black, the clouds are low, and it's stormy. The winds are blowing, but the little bird is sleeping with its little beak in its breast. He is sleeping in the midst of the storm because he's in the crevice of a rock.

Jesus is the rock in a weary land. When you nestle yourself into His presence, no amount of wind or rain, no storm in your life can harm you. You will be safe in the crevice of the Rock. In the crevice there is rest for the weary soul. The Lord wants us to learn how to live in a restful spirit. I'm not talking about going to bed, going to sleep, or going home to be with the Lord. He says, "Come to Me, and I will give you rest—all of you who work so hard beneath a heavy yoke" (Mt. 11:28). Each saint of God needs to learn how to rest in God. The only way you rest in God is to trust Him completely and say, "Lord, I'm in Your hands. All that I do is in Your hands and I cast all my cares on You."

People will brand you when you start resting in your spirit. They will brand you when you stop worrying and don't give in to anxiety anymore. When you are able to put your spirit at rest in Christ, the world will call you uncaring. If you lose one of your loved ones and you don't cry a whole lot, scream, and hang all over the casket, they will say you are callous. They don't realize that you understand the process. You know your loved one has moved from one dimension to another and you don't need to scream and panic. You can rest in the midst of your sorrow.

It's called resting when you've lost your job of 25 years and you smile. You're supposed to be crying and pulling your hair out of your head. But you can say, "The Lord gave me that job and He can give me another one. And while I'm waiting, I'm going to rest, for I know the next one will be better than the first." You know the job is not your source. God is your source. Some things don't happen overnight. There are some circumstances that take time to change. But you can't panic. You must learn to trust God and rest in His salvation, saying, "I behold the Lord. He strengthens me, sustains me, holds me up, and keeps me going. He is my source and He is my strength. I'm resting in the midst of the storm because I've learned how to trust God." That's what God is trying to get across to you. If we are to be lights to the community and to the world, we've got to act like we know everything is all right. All is well in the midst of problems. If we're going to cry and panic and go somewhere and have a pity party, how are we any different from the world? Why would they want to listen to us? How can we introduce them to the Lord, if we don't trust Him?

The Bible tells us to cast all our care on Him because He cares for us (see 1 Pet. 5:7). The Lord knows everything that is going to happen to you and, if you stay in tune with God, He's already prepared a way for you. It is important to maintain your prayer life and to be faithful to meditate on His Word. He will prepare you for what you've got to face and then when it comes upon you, you will be surprised how easily you go through it, praising the Lord in spite of it. When you trust God, you can praise God, if you don't have any money. You can praise God if you don't know where your next meal is coming from. You can praise God if you've had a broken relationship. You can praise God if things have turned sour on you because you know God has you in His hand.

You've got to get to the point where you can say, "I will bless the Lord at all times: His praise shall continually be in my mouth" (Ps. 34:1 KJV). It's just good to have His presence in you. I don't have to wait for Sunday to be with Him. I don't have to wait to feel His presence. I don't have to wait to praise Him. I don't have to wait to trust Him.

Wherever I go, He goes with me. His praises will continually be in my mouth. You can't trust flesh. God didn't tell us to trust flesh. He said, "Put no confidence in flesh" (see Phil. 3:3). You can't even trust your own flesh, but you can trust God in you. When you trust God in you, He can sustain you and keep you safe. When you trust God, you won't be disappointed. When people act crazy and strange and they mistreat you, if you keep your mind on the Lord and say, "I'm trusting God," you won't be disturbed. In order to trust God, though, we have to stay focused. How do we stay focused? We keep our minds on the right thing. We keep our minds on the principles of God.

Paul's letter to the Philippians encourages us to think on those things that are lovely, think on those things of good report, and think on those things that are pure (see Phil. 4:8). You've got to think right if you want to really feel the presence of God. If you don't think right, you're going to feel frustration, pain, hate, and disharmony. You've got to focus on the Lord. The Lord said, "I will keep in perfect peace those whose mind is stayed on Me, because they trust Me" (see Is. 26:3). If I want God's presence to be manifested in my life, if I want the harmony of God to be manifested in my life, I've got to keep my mind focused on God.

There are many distractions in this world. Often it is not easy to stay focused. Even when you're praying, the enemy will bring up worldly problems. He says, "Your bills are due. You've got this to pay," and all the while you're trying to pray and say, "Lord, help me." You realize that there are bills to pay and things that you must get done. Therefore, at times such as these it is difficult to stay focused. But like anything worthwhile, you must practice focusing on God every day. Find ways to affirm your faith and trust. Read the Scriptures. Order your words to say, "The Lord is my light and my salvation; whom shall I fear? God is with me and in me and around me. I shall not want for anything. He is my shepherd and my best friend. He surrounds me with an army of angels and my enemies fall by my side."

When you feel like you're down and out and you can't make it, listen to what the Lord says. He's the lifter of your soul and of your head (see Ps. 3:3). Trust God; read what He says He will do for you. He's dependable, isn't He? I believe that everything will work together for good, just as Paul said in Romans 8:28. I don't always understand how things work. I thought I would understand everything all the time. Paul says that there are some things we will never understand, but I know that God is causing the good to come out of the worst of circumstances. God is in your life and He's concerned about you.

When you woke up, did you hear the voice of God say, "I love you"? Did you tell Him, "I love you too"? Doesn't it make a difference when you can have a communion like that with God? The Lord said to me the other day, when I was preparing myself for a service, "I want you to tell My people to trust Me, not with their lips, but with their actions." When you trust God, you have a better life and a more secure life. You will live the abundant life. That doesn't mean you will have a lot of money. But you will have peace in your spirit and in your mind. Then you will not be walking around frustrated, disturbed, anxious, and worried.

There are so many things happening. We've got to meet all kinds of challenges. But when you really count on God, He'll sustain you every time. People will be wondering, how can you make it? You can witness and say, "It's God in me who brought victory my way." When there is nothing else left but God, He is more than enough. If everything collapsed, if all things went into a tailspin, you can still count on God. He is going to look out for you. He really loves you. He really cares for you. God loves you more than you can imagine. He's been there all the time with you. Even when you didn't recognize Him, He was there. He's been making ways for you when you didn't even recognize it. Now you can look back and say, "Look what the Lord brought me out of." Don't let the devil take you back to where you were. Don't let him put you in dark dungeons. Step up on the mountain of faith and declare that God is your strength, your salvation, your hope, your power, your encouragement, and your supply. All you need is in God and you can rest in that fact and do well.

Will you declare that in your spirit? I have nothing to worry about, for I trust God. The God who made the moon and the stars, the God who makes the earth His footstool, the God who put the stars in their places, is the God whom I serve. The God who put breath in my body, the God who heals me when I'm sick, the God who puts food on my table, is the One whom I trust. What about you? I'll trust Him till I die. In order to trust Him, you have to trust Jesus, for Jesus brings the Father's presence into your soul. To reject Him is to reject the presence of the Father. That's how the Lord became intimate with us. Through Jesus, He came and identified with us as human beings. Jesus came for you and me and He paid the price for our sins. Then the Father gave Him back to us as a gift. If you accepted the Gift, then He lives in you. Through Jesus, we received the Holy Ghost and with Him as our Comforter and Guide, we become fiery flames, lights in the world, cities that sit on the hill and cannot be ignored.

Chapter 8

There Is a Miracle at Your Fingertips

The Role of Faith

Elisha replied, "The Lord says that by this time tomorrow two gallons of flour or four gallons of barley grain will be sold in the markets of Samaria for a dollar!" The officer assisting the king said, "That couldn't happen if the Lord made windows in the sky!" But Elisha replied, "You will see it happen, but you won't be able to buy any of it!" Now there were four lepers sitting outside the city gates. "Why sit here unto we die?" they asked each other. We will starve if we stay here and we will starve if we go back into the city; so we might as well go out and surrender to the Syrian army. If they let us live, so much the better; but if they kill us, we would have died anyway." So that evening they went out to the camp of the Syrians, but there was no one there! (For the Lord had made the whole Syrian army hear the clatter of speeding chariots and a loud galloping of horses and the sounds of a great army approaching "The king of Israel has hired the Hittites and Egyptians to attack us," they cried out. So they panicked and fled into the night, abandoning their tents, horses, donkeys, and everything else.) When the lepers arrived at the edge of the camp they went into one tent after another, eating, drinking wine, and carrying out silver and gold and clothing and hiding it (2 Kings 7:1-8).

Do you sometimes feel that God has run out of power? How many of you will admit that at times you have felt that God has just run out of power and abandoned you? Perhaps you feel He is no longer interested in what happens to you. You see, sometimes people all around you give Him praise and you wonder, "Lord, have You forgotten me? I'm one of Your children too." Maybe you believe, deep down inside of you, that there is a God, but you just need to know how to contact Him.

When you believe God, you are within fingertip-reach of a miracle, and it will be yours according to your faith. This Scripture from Second Kings 7 deals with the next 24 hours of your life.

The events described in this text happened in a 24-hour period. One day the situation seemed hopeless and the next day there was a miraculous solution to the problem. This passage demonstrates the need to hold on to hope. It is never too late to receive your miracle, if you act now.

In this story a great famine had swept the land of Samaria. No matter how rich you were, no matter if you had all the money in the world, you could not purchase food. There was no flour or barley to make bread. Elisha, the prophet, proclaimed the Word of the Lord to the people. "Tomorrow about this same time," he said, "in 24 hours, for a few pennies you can buy all you need." An officer who assisted the king sort of scoffed and got sarcastic. He spoke out of his unbelief and said that even if God opened a window from Heaven, this prophecy would not come to pass. You always have those people who scoff at God's messenger. They get sarcastic when you talk and walk in faith. You see God doing the impossible; they only see the impossible. What man calls impossible, God calls possible.

This man had never seen a solution like the one the prophet was announcing. Because he had not seen it before, he refused to believe it could happen. He was holding on to physical sight based on past events. Elisha was seeing with his spiritual sight based on God's promise. So when the prophet heard the man's scoffing, he looked him eyeball to eyeball and replied, "You'll see it, but you won't eat of it. You won't be around to eat of it." Just as the prophet had predicted, the man was trampled at the gate as the people rushed out to gather the food left by the Syrians (see 2 Kings 7:17). When a prophet speaks, a prophet of God, you can count on it.

We don't often realize how much God wants to fight our battles and supply our needs. In this story, the people assumed they were about to die, either from starvation or at the hands of the mighty Syrian army. In the midst of all this despair, four lepers, who were outside the gates of the city, made a decision. As they talked among themselves, they decided to do something other than sit and wait for death to come. They were already outcasts. The disease of leprosy was worse than today's AIDS. At least, if you have AIDS, you are in contact with people other than those who have AIDS. You can shake hands with them, you can sit beside them and hug them. You may believe the myth that those with AIDS should be treated like the lepers of old, but this simply is ignorance on your part. But in biblical times, lepers were isolated from family, friends, and community. Those who were afflicted with leprosy were required to let everyone know they had the disease by continually crying out, "Unclean, unclean, I'm a leper, I'm a leper."

So, these four were sitting together because they all had the same condition. You can't catch what you already have. They said, "Why do we sit here until we die? We will starve if we stay here. And we will starve if we go into the city because the famine is in the city.

We may as well go to the camp of the Syrian army. If they spare us, we shall live. If they kill us, we would have died anyway. This is a no-win situation, so we might as well take our chances." The four lepers went out at twilight into the camp of the Syrian army. But when they entered the camp, they found no one there. While everyone was sinking deeper and deeper into their despair, the Lord fooled the Syrian army into thinking a great army was approaching. He caused them to hear the noises of horses and chariots and they fled in fear. By the time the lepers arrived, the camp was empty.

How mighty is the God I serve? He is always in control. He can create the sounds of a great army and make it sound so real that the greatest army in the world will give up the fight and flee in terror. God said that He will take the riches from the wicked and put it in the hands of the righteous (see Prov. 13:22). Some of you have failed to grasp this truth. But there are some of you who, having seen God work in your life, know that His miracle-working power is alive and well. God has given you jobs that folks said you would never get. They were removed from the hands of folk who didn't respect Him and given to you. If you acknowledge God and give God your heart and delight in Him, He'll give you the desires of your heart. Some of you have been promoted ahead of those who didn't even think you would get the job to begin with. They talked about you, said what you wouldn't do, and how you wouldn't make it, and now you are their supervisor. God can change things around for your good.

You may not know how you got your job or your promotion, and I don't know how God made these sounds so real to the Syrian army. All I know is they heard something that brought fear into their hearts and they ran, leaving everything they owned behind. There were no chariots, no horses, no army approaching; only the sound. Often what we cannot see is more fearful than what we can see.

This great Bible story may seem a long time in the past. Actually, through the Holy Spirit, it is closer than you think. It may even deal with the very moment in which you live. In the next 24 hours of your life, a mighty miracle may come to you, bringing God's miraculous supply into your life to take care of your need or your hurt. Here's how the next 24 hours can change your life. There was a time when these four lepers needed a miracle. They had a need that could not be filled by human intervention. There was no reason to even imagine that such a miracle could take place. In fact, when the prophet said that in 24 hours there would be a major miracle, people had a hard time accepting it. But Elisha knew God didn't need a week, a month, or a year to change the situation. When God told Elisha to tell the people "24 hours," Elisha knew they would not have to wait any longer than one full day.

Some folk reading this can hardly believe what I'm saying. That's because they have never put their complete trust in God. Whatever your need, say, "Lord, it's in Your hands" and in 24 hours a difference can take place. This is what it is all about. Elisha reminded the king's assistant, who mocked him, that God will provide a miracle and there will be plenty of food by tomorrow. He would never have a chance to eat it, but the food would be there. I want to tell you straight from my heart to yours that there is a dividing line between faith and doubt. There is a difference between a person who believes God for miracles and a person who doubts.

A dear friend of this ministry, Bishop Jeff Banks of Newark, New Jersey, used to say, "You can believe God and receive, or doubt and be without." If you are without today, you better get rid of doubt. If you want to see God manifest things in your life, you better start trusting Him and believe in His Word. You must stand on His Word and realize that God doesn't lie. If God says something to you, He will fulfill it. It may take time, but God will manifest every promise He's made. You know, you pay an awful price for doubt. You miss out on God's miracles, you miss out on the nearness and closeness of God in your life, and you don't have a sense of the presence of the Lord, which brings abundance instead of mere existence.

Living outside of the presence of God is to live in doubt and fear, and frustration and discouragement. To those who choose to bless the Lord and praise His name, there is peace, love, and a sound mind. I decided long ago to exchange my complaints for praise. Did you praise Him this morning or did you complain? Did you wake up with a frown on your face or did you have a smile in your heart? Have you told Him "I love You," instead of thinking about your problems? If you keep your mind on your problems, you'll go down the tube. But if you keep your eyes on God, you'll rise to praise.

What comes to your mind when you read a story like this one about the victory over the Syrian army? Do you believe it can happen today, that things can really change in 24 hours? Perhaps you don't think these were real people. They were as real as you and me, but you may say, "Did they face what I face, Pastor?" Have you ever been so hungry that you wanted to eat you own child? The Bible tells us that they were hungry enough to eat their own children (see 2 Kings 6:24-30). People will do desperate things when they are faced with imminent death. I have talked to Vietnam veterans who told me they were so thirsty they drank water from pools of water filled with dead people. If you've never been really hungry or really thirsty, you can't relate to such behavior.

When there isn't enough, you can't be picky about what you eat. If you are hungry enough, it doesn't matter whether you like it or not, you will eat it. Even if you don't like brussel sprouts, you will eat them. The reason you're so choosy is that you're not hungry enough. The same is true with clothes. When you are standing naked in the cold, you'll accept anything to wear.

The famine was so bad in Samaria that many had turned to cannibalism, eating their own children and their neighbor's children. You may have money, but money won't satisfy your hunger. These were real people with real struggles. Yes, they needed a miracle they couldn't believe for, but the prophet Elisha knew something those people needed to know. Elisha knew that God was going to intervene. If you believe, God can intervene for you. Without a single arrow being shot, God drove the enemy out of their camp.

Elisha knew a spiritual truth and he was trying to change the people's attitude and get them into a spirit of receptivity. If you are going to receive something, you have to get an attitude adjustment. If you are expecting God to do something special for you, you need to start rejoicing now. Don't wait until after the fact to shout. Begin the celebration now.

When you promise your children something, they get excited by the promise. The reason they get excited when they hear the promise is they believe in your word. They believe you will do what you say. They go to shouting and saying, "Thank you, Mommy; thank you, Dad." They don't have what you promised yet, but they know you will fulfill your promise and that is good enough for them.

God wants you to react like your children do. Jesus said that the Kingdom of God is based on childlike faith (see Mk. 10:15-16). If children believe you are going to take them to an amusement park, they will be filled with excitement even though you haven't started the car yet. Their heads are filled with visions of Ferris wheels and roller coasters. They have rides on the brain. You should be that excited when God promises you that He's going to take you to new dimensions. You should get ready for the ride. You should see the end in your mind, even though there is no evidence that God has begun to act on your behalf.

When we get desperate, we think God is a million miles away. We are hurt, we feel pain, and we feel alone. It's hard to conceive that God can heal us either by medicine or by prayer. If we get low in our finances and have very little money, we sometimes can't conceive of the fact that God can put money into our hands. We just don't see the miracle. Even though we are supposed to look to God as our source, seldom do we consider that as we struggle with our problem. He can put money in your hand when it looks impossible. God can put money in your hand from the most unexpected source. You get checks unexpectedly when you learn how to live on the level of faith where you know God is your source. You'll get a refund check that you never would have received if you hadn't put your faith in God. God can touch the bank's computer. You'll look in your checking account and you'll see a balance where there should be a zero. God knew you needed a miracle.

He can make that person, who has owed you money for ten years, come up and pay you. You have been limiting God and if you take the limits off of God, you will be amazed at what He has in store for you. God is just waiting to give you more. It is His pleasure to give you the Kingdom (see Lk. 12:32). If you seek the Kingdom first, He will throw in the rest (see Mt. 6:33). When you are hurt or being hurt, it is hard to believe God is with you. For those of you who are hurting today, I encourage you to trust God. You can't give up.

Take care not to fall into a pity party. You may groan and moan and say that you don't deserve anything from God. Most of us who do get blessed don't deserve it. Fortunately, it isn't about deserving. It's about God's goodness and mercy. I don't tell the Lord what I deserve or that He owes me something. Instead, I thank Him for what He does because I know it's His grace. I know He can withhold some things. He can shut up the heavens. But if you trust Him, He'll open the windows of Heaven and pour out a blessing you won't have room enough to receive (see Mal. 3:10).

The enemy is a liar who will try to plant a seed of doubt in your mind. He'll tell you that God can't do it or that He's forgotten you. He wants you to think, in the midst of your hurt, that God is not around. That's why you need to carry Him inside you, everywhere you go. He said, "Lo, I am with you always" (Mt. 28:20). God has no difficulty performing miracles. He spoke to the prophet and said that about this time tomorrow every need the people have will be supplied. All God was waiting for was someone to believe that He is the source. All He needs is for you to look to Him as the source and believe. He is the supplier. He doesn't need your help. He isn't concerned with your ability. He is only concerned with your availability.

Is there a problem you have been wrestling with for years? You've been trying to do something about it and you haven't made any progress. What are you going to do about it? I don't know what you are going to do about your problem, but I'm going to turn mine over to the Lord. I believe if I turn it over to the Lord, He can do more with it than I can. Once you turn it over to the Lord, don't think about it anymore, for if you think about it, you will try to figure it out. While you're figuring it out, God can't work it out. But when you stop figuring it out, God can work it out.

I'm one of the men of the twentieth century who believes that God is a God of miracles. I believe when we come to the end of our way that God's way is there to pick us up. I believe that when we run out of something, we should start giving and expect everything we need to be supplied. We can receive what God has for us. It is not too late to receive, if we act now. The next 24 hours can be your miracle receiving time.

It's interesting that the men who acted and who really picked up on the Word of God were the most unlikely candidates. In this case they were lepers. They were sitting at the gate, afflicted with an incurable disease and starving to death. These men surely won't pay any attention to the prophet. They are diseased and their flesh is all messed up. They won't listen to a preacher. Why try to tell them that tomorrow about this time it will be all right? Their reply might be, "Don't you know I have leprosy? Don't you know I'm hurting? Don't you know I lost my family? Don't you know that I am an outcast?" What is your complaint? Are you complaining about your children who have run away, your son who is in jail, your daughter who is strung out on cocaine? Are you complaining about your marriage, a divorce, your best friend who deceived you?

You may not even know why you are reading this book, but I know why. You are looking for an answer to your problem and the Holy Ghost knows you need to hear what I have to say. I, Jonathan Greer II, say that about this time tomorrow you can look for your miracle. You can receive it if you want or you can doubt and be without. I have something else to tell you. God loves you so much that He put this message on my heart for you. He knows what you have been going through. God knows that you need some hope. Who knows what you might do without hope. The enemy may tell you to kill yourself. You tell him he's a liar. There is hope for you.

These men were hurting badly, but they listened and the message of the prophet Elisha reached them. They felt in their spirits that God was going to do something great. They didn't know how. But they started by asking the question, "Why do we sit here? Why in the world are we going to sit here and pity ourselves till we die?"

You ought to take a chance with God instead of sitting still. Get up and walk on His promise. These lepers may have felt foolish walking toward the camp of the enemy, expecting God to perform a miracle. People may think you're out of your mind when you do what seems to be foolish things. But you're in your right mind, if you start moving forth in faith and expecting to receive a miracle from God. God looked down and saw those four men stumbling along. Nobody would have called that a march of faith except God. But He saw men who believed it could be done.

So many people have talked themselves into believing that their problems can't be solved or their needs can't be met. Sometimes it's a wonderful thing not to be so smart. It is simpler to believe that God is God and that you can receive a miracle.

I want to encourage you to believe today and use your faith. God has told you through this story that there's a miracle for you. He's told you that the next 24 hours will be your life-changing experience. He's told you there's going to be a breakthrough. He told you that Heaven is getting ready to open up for you. He's told you to look to the hills for your help, for all help comes from the Lord.

Chapter 9

God: Watchful and Faithful

God Watches Over His Creation

If it wasn't for the Lord watching over us, the trials and tribulations of life would have destroyed us by now. It is comforting and encouraging to know that God's eye is watching over us. God wants you to prosper in all areas of your life. What you must understand, though, is just because it is His desire for you to prosper does not mean that you won't have to go through some difficult periods. All of the saints of God, those who stand with God and walk close with Him and are getting deeper into the revelation of God, have also been going through conflict. To be saved, filled with His Spirit, and anointed to do ministry, does not exempt you from conflict. Surely, they that live Godly in Christ shall suffer persecution.

They that trust in the Lord shall be as mount Zion, which cannot be removed, but abideth for ever. As the mountains are round about Jerusalem, so the Lord is round about His people from henceforth even for ever. For the rod of the wicked shall not rest upon the lot of the righteous; lest the righteous put forth their hands unto iniquity. Do good, O Lord, unto those that be good, and to them that are upright in their hearts. As for such as turn aside unto their crooked ways, the Lord shall lead them forth with the workers of iniquity: but peace shall be upon Israel (Psalm 125 KJV).

Israel, in this Psalm, represents the people of God and, as His children, that includes you and me. The words recorded here by the psalmist tells us that the Lord's presence is in and around the people of God just like the mountains are around Jerusalem. When you go into Jerusalem, you can see, from a distance, the mountains that surround the city. As sure as they stand and continue to stand, the presence of God surrounds God's people.

God's presence also lives in His people to keep them from moving and to hold them steadfast in spite of what they go through. The Lord will not allow a wicked ruler to come in and rule over His people because the wicked ruler may try to lead them away from Him. In and of themselves, they would not be able to stand. God provides a righteous ruler for His people so they will keep their eyes on Him.

Recently, as I was considering the things God was about to do through me and through the people of my congregation, the enemy launched an attack on me. It was so strong in the spirit, it affected me physically, as if someone had hit me in the stomach. I was gasping for breath and I felt so weak in the face of this blow from satan. In the midst of the attack, praises came out of my heart and I gave the battle over to the Lord. Being a pastor or a leader doesn't exempt one from conflict. It is all in how you respond to the attack. When I get hit with something, it draws me closer to the Father and makes me know that God is watching over me. As our choir often sings, "He is the Lifter of my head." Just when it seems as if my head will be pushed into the dirt, God's Spirit has a way of lifting my head above the problems or conflict.

Those who never go through anything can't take it. You can't be close to God if you haven't gone through suffering, for when you're riding on easy street you relax. You turn away from God when you have things going your way, but when you have to go through problems, troubles, and pressures, it makes you aware that if God is not for you, you can't make it. The Spirit reminds you that no weapon formed against you will prosper (see Is. 54:17). The weapons that satan is forming against God's people are like forged checks. They won't make it through the system because they don't have the right signature. If one or two make it through, they won't prosper because the bank will make the error good.

The enemy tries to draw your spirit away from God and tries to destroy your courage. He tries to draw on your spiritual account, but his efforts won't last. He only makes it work for a season. God's got a time and a way to pull and snatch the weapons out of his hand. I believe that those who trust in the Lord are as steady as Mount Zion. They are not moved by any circumstance. That doesn't mean you're not touched or sensitive to things that happen to you. But you don't move. You will not be moved. You will not be wiped away and blown away. You will be like a tree planted by the rivers of water when you trust in God and His power to get you through the attack.

We ought to pray for each other more. We ought to stop talking so much and start praying. Try praying more when you can sense God's people in need. Feel one another's burdens and hurts. When we start sharing, we can all make it a lot better for each other. It is better to work together than to work against each other.

The angels of God are encamped around those who fear and respect God (see Ps. 34:7). You don't see them with your natural eyes, but they are on the job. When you need help and you aren't sure who to call on, the ministering angels will come to your aid. If you can't see the road ahead of your car, faith in God will take you home safely because the angels go before you to make a way. If you have the faith when you're walking down the dark streets, you won't fear a mugger because you are carrying the presence of God. God will protect you as you go through the streets and if a man or woman tries to harm you, the Holy Ghost will lift up a standard against their evil actions. When you come, God comes with you and when you go, God goes with you.

Another thing we need to do more is to praise God in the midst of trouble. You don't need to wait until you get to church to praise God. You won't know how to lift the banner of praise in a time of trouble if you only praise God once a week. That's why some of you are cold when you go to church. You haven't praised Him every morning and every evening. If you go to church with praises in your heart, you'll come in the door saying, "Thank You, Lord. One more day, one more time I can come and be around people who love the Lord." There is no greater thrill than to be in the midst of people who are primed from a week of praising Him.

A recent radio program told of six or seven police officers in Washington, D.C. that started singing in a quartet at their precinct. They said the reason they started it was they needed the fellowship. Their job was filled with stress and they used singing as a way of relief. When they would come into the prison, the prisoners would ask them to sing. So they locked them up and sang the gospel to them to get them saved.

My point is, you need to come to church. Don't tell me you can do without regular attendance; it's the fellowship that is important. It's being in the same room with people, who are of one mind and one spirit, praising God at one time. Together the people shake the heavens and open the doors for you. When you leave church, God has already gone before you. The praises have come up before Him and He won't ignore His people.

Psalm 34 tells us His praises shall continue. You notice it says, "His praises," not "your praises." Many are not able to offer praises to God because they only praise Him when they have received something good. That's human praise. The praise that comes out when you're suffering and you don't have what you need, but your still praising God is the continual praise I am talking about. You must simply open up and the Holy Ghost will praise God through your lips. God's praises shall continually be in my mouth and I'll bless Him at all times (see Ps. 34:1). I'll bless Him and He'll be glorified through me.

The third verse of Psalm 125 refers to the wicked, who shall not rule over the Godly lest the Godly be forced to do wrong. God will not let wicked leaders rule over His Godly people. I believe you will begin to see a trend. Some of these employers who are ungodly and who have mistreated their employees down through the years are going to experience God's power. God will remove them and put Godly people in charge. Be prepared for God to move the wicked out of a position of power and to replace them with righteous men and women. These righteous will not only perform better at the job, they will be witnesses to those who are still a part of the world.

God's work in the Old Testament is our example. He let the people of God take everything the enemy had. Those who didn't fall in battle were run out of town. They left the silver, the gold, and all their possessions. All God's people had to do was walk in and set up housekeeping. They didn't have to build a house or buy a herd. They went from "rice and beans" to land, silver, and gold.

That is the trend I see beginning to take shape now. That's why the economy is shaking. It's in the danger zone, but the politicians won't say anything about it. No one is sure what will happen, but I can tell you that in the end God's way will prevail. The country may be bankrupt, but God's Kingdom is filled to overflowing with milk and honey. The experts can't manage the country because they can't even manage their own lives. If you can't manage to live a Godly life, you can't manage people. When God brings this country to its knees, those who are in tune with God, the holy and Godly people, will go through open doors and reap what they didn't sow.

Many of you are sitting in a house you didn't build. You let somebody else build it for you and you just moved right in. How many of you were surprised when you got your house? You never dreamed you would be where you are today. Saints ought to give God the credit. He gave you your house. I don't care how much money you did or didn't have, God gave you that house and you ought to praise Him for it every time you walk in it. Don't take it for granted.

There are folks sitting out on the street with no place to live. You ought to shout, "Thank You, Lord." You have money you thought you would never have. It may not be a whole lot right now, but it's a whole lot more than you used to have. I used to live on 50 dollars a week. I was blessed with a place to live. A wonderful woman gave me a room in her house when I preached in New Jersey. I couldn't afford a hotel. As an evangelist, I received what the people were able to give. Often it rained and attendance was poor. I would preach all night, every night, and my share of the offering would be no more than 60 or 70 dollars a week. But I knew God would meet my needs and that kept a smile on my face. I made it a point to continually praise God. He was faithful to do more than I could have ever asked.

Some of you had to pay your way through school. I think you probably got better grades than most other folks. When you have to work your way through school, you can't spend time playing around. When your tuition is due, you can't look to mama and papa or grandpa and grandma or auntie. Whatever you achieved, you achieved because God was with you. You shouldn't flaunt your achievements, for it is God who deserves the glory. Thank God for what you've done and find ways to help and encourage others to trust in Him. Be an ambassador for Him and help someone else along the way. The more you help people, the more God will bless you. The more you put out, the more He'll return to you.

If you give a cup of cold water to somebody, do it from your heart. God will give you a well of water in return. Here's an example of how three men at Cathedral of Faith Church exemplified brotherly love. The other day, Brother Butler went by Brother Bell's house. He gave Brother Bell his brand new coat. He pulled it off his back and gave it to him. Then, Brother Butler said, "Now I need one too. I'm cold." A few nights later Brother Nealy knocked on his door and gave him a new coat. Brother Butler came in shouting to me, "Pastor, Brother Nealy gave me his coat. We saints ought to learn how to share with each other." If you see somebody without a coat, give them yours. God will give you five more.

Furthermore, why don't you try what I am doing? I am emptying my closet and getting rid of things. I'm not talking about rags, either. I'm getting ready to give some of my brothers my clothes. When you do that, the Lord puts twice as much back in your closet. You have to give it away again the next month. Some of you ought to try it this week. Clean out the closet, get the best you got in there, and give it to somebody who needs it. Don't give away rags. If you don't want it, nobody else will either. It's the same with food. When you donate food, make sure the food is something you would like to eat too. If you don't eat canned goods, don't bring canned goods to the donation center. If you eat canned goods, then bring them. But if you eat fresh fruits and vegetables, then bring fresh fruits and vegetables.

Psalm 125:4 tells us to do good to those who are good, whose hearts are right with the Lord. That's what the Lord is going to do. That's a principle. Those who do good will have good done to them. You bring on yourself what you yourself put out. God isn't killing anyone. Your own sins are killing you. It is sin that destroys you; God is not a destroyer of His people.

In Psalm 125:5 we are shown the consequences of turning aside from doing good. Those who follow a crooked way will be led by the Lord to join the workers of iniquity. This is another way to say, "You reap what you sow" (see Gal. 6:7). It is God's desire to bring only good into your life, things that will help you live a life full of joy. Good will come to those who do good, but those who choose evil will be surrounded by evil. They are going where they are supposed to go—to their own execution. People who practice evil end up as their own executioners. If you practice evil, no good will come upon you.

Those who go around hurting folks and destroying people will see the same come back to them. You don't have to fight them. You need to stop worrying about folks who mistreat you. Just don't fellowship with them. I won't fellowship with you if you hurt me every time I'm around you. I can speak to you and love you through my prayers for you, but I am not going to allow you to beat on me with your words and deeds.

Unfortunately, this is often the case within families. Those who should love and accept you without condition are often guilty of causing you the most grief. It is a hard thing to say, but you may have to refuse to have a relationship with some family members. Whether it is your brother or sister, blood doesn't always have anything to do with how you are treated. Sometimes you are treated with more kindness and you are closer to people in your church than you are to your own brothers and sisters.

I refuse to go into a stress-filled atmosphere. Why should I take myself through all those changes? When you are hurt by your mother or your father or any of your family, the best way to deal with them is through prayer. Pray for them and love them.

You don't have to stay with anyone who doesn't want you and who treats you badly. I don't care if you are married to them. I don't believe you should stay in a relationship that is like living in hell every day. You have to get away from each other to cool off. Sometimes you have to get away to get a perspective on the relationship. When you step back from a problem and take time to analyze it, you often see a way to solve it. If you are sincere in your heart and do good, the Lord will honor your efforts and work with you and through you to heal the relationship.

At the end of Psalm 125:5 the psalmist prays for Israel to have quietness and peace. Israel represents the people of God, so this prayer is for you too. God wants every one of you to enjoy your life. Live the life you love and love the life you live.

Once you are saved and sanctified by the Holy Ghost, there is no need to continue in confusion and frustration. Doesn't that make sense? I don't have to feel bound every time I come to church. I refuse that kind of life style. I choose to rejoice. I choose to praise God. I choose to be happy. I choose not to worry. Whatever I am faced with, I'm still going to trust the Lord, for God has everything in His hands. My footsteps are ordered by God.

I know you've been hit with some things; I know you're going to be hit with some more things, but I'm trying to prepare you to learn how to deal with them by rejoicing always. Three or four years ago the Lord moved upon me with a special anointing in order to equip me for a situation which He knew was to come upon me. Had He not stepped into my life in that very powerful way at that time, I feel confident in saying that I would not have been able to handle what happened to me. The Lord always equips you for the conflict. He never puts more on you than you can bear. You can say, "This is too much for me." You can say it and complain all you want to, but God knows what He is doing. It's just that you aren't willing to go through the experience of the preparation process. It's like Jesus said when He felt the pressure: "If it be possible, let this cup pass from Me" (see Mt. 26:39). His human side said, "I don't want to take it. I don't want to take it." But then the spirit cried out, "Nevertheless not My will, but Thine, be done" (see Lk. 22:42). It's a cup filled with a brew that you don't want to taste. I didn't want to drink from this cup, but I had to drink. God sustained me with His power and I felt more of His strength in the midst of my anguish than I would have felt if I had never faced it. As a result, I am more aware of God's presence in me.

I Am Courageous and Victorious

Deuteronomy 31:6 KJV tells us, "Be strong and of a good courage, fear not, nor be afraid of them: for the Lord thy God, He it is that doth go with thee; He will not fail thee, nor forsake thee." Moses told the children of Israel this when he was getting ready to turn the reins over to Joshua. They were reluctant about this new leadership. He said, "Listen, I'm not going over to the Promised Land, but I'm going to tell you something before I leave you. Be strong and be of good courage." He told Joshua the same thing—to be strong and be of good courage.

The Lord told me to say that I am courageous and victorious. Don't talk about being defeated. Don't look at your appearances. Don't worry about opposition. Be courageous. Overcome the negative and annoying habits through your faith-filled prayer life. Learn how to spend quality time each day with the Lord so you'll know that you are victorious.

The Lord wants you to abandon weak, whimpering, chicken-like attitudes. He wants you to grasp hold of an eagle attitude. Saints, you have to take charge now. You've been sitting in the valley too long, complaining too much, attending too many pity parties. When the world needs strength—sanctified strength—you're too busy with your physical condition. The saints of God have to stand up and take charge in the spirit and say, "I'm victorious and I'm courageous." God's army has no cowardly soldiers. He's given you the victory already.

The victory is in Jesus. You're not defeated at all. You experience victory after victory after victory. You experience victory because you're a part of a victorious host of saints. Saints don't lose battles because the battle is the Lord's. Saints experience the victory by winning every battle. Even though you don't have to fight the battle, the Lord allows you to experience the victory.

You can celebrate another of God's victories over satan. He has given you power over him, but without a battle, there would never be a victory. Often God allows you to go through the darkness first, then He gives you some sunny days. You cannot know healing until you have experienced sickness. You don't know the benefits of God's provisions for your life until you have gone through financial reverses. God lets you go

God: Watchful and Faithful

through some negative things so He can show you the positive side of Himself. God allows evil so He can give you good.

In the midst of your fiery furnace, in the midst of your lion's den, in the midst of your valley, God makes you victorious. You must be courageous and you must not back up from satan. You are going to step on his head again and again because you are victorious. Sometimes those knocks stop you. Sometimes you shake a little bit. Sometimes you reel and rock, but God says, "If you get pressed down, I'll pick you up." It is God who is able to keep you from falling and to present you faultless before the throne of His glory (see Jude 24).

I want you to know that courage is a quality of mind and heart. This is a precious heritage that our heavenly Father has given to us. Whenever and whatever we need, we must go forth with courage. Whenever you need strength, God's grace is there for you and His grace is more than sufficient. Ten years ago He didn't let you go through a lot of things because you weren't ready for them. But now you are ready. He said, "You can take it now." You may not want to, but you can take it because you have courage and you will be victorious.

As you experience the victory of more and more battles, you will mature in the Lord. He can give you more and more responsibility because He knows you will trust Him to bring you through. Through all of these victories, you will be building your testimony for the Lord. Some of us run out of testimony. That's why we keep saying the same thing over again. When you keep going through some battles and keep coming out victorious, you have some brand-new testimonies.

If you are sanctified by the Holy Ghost, it is time you graduated. You are set apart for service and it is time you started to serve. Has God done something more than just save you? Salvation is the greatest gift, but there is more He's done since He saved you. I have come through many dangers and snares. I had my dark days and my hard days. God has given me victory after victory.

When the enemy comes again, ask him what he's got up his sleeve this time. Then tell him that whatever he has planned will not prevail. He may want to destroy you, but you have the experience of victory behind you. Tell him to go ahead and try. Tell him to give it his best shot. The Lord had to let him loose on you because he couldn't come to you unless He let him loose. The Lord can stop him any time He wants. If God lets him loose, He must have a purpose in mind. Tell satan that he may as well do what he is going to do quickly, because you already have the victory.

Every time you go through a little skirmish, you emerge from the battle with a testimony. So testify to His goodness and make known His deeds among the people. Testify while you can. Praise God while you can, because you don't know when the end is. You ought to praise God every day you live, for when you go home, you want to go home praising God.

Chapter 10

The Steadfast Love of the Lord Never Ceases

God Will Always Be There

So he got up and ate and drank. Strengthened by that food, he traveled forty days and forty nights until he reached Horeb, the mountain of God. There he went into a cave and spent the night. And the word of the Lord came to him: "What are you doing here, Elijah?" He replied, "I have been very zealous for the Lord God Almighty. The Israelites have rejected Your covenant, broken down Your altars, and put Your prophets to death with the sword. I am the only one left, and now they are trying to kill me too." The Lord said, "Go out and stand on the mountain in the presence of the Lord for the Lord is about to pass by." Then a great and powerful wind tore the mountains apart and shattered the rocks before the Lord, but the Lord was not in the wind. After the wind there was an earthquake, but the Lord was not in the earthquake. After the earthquake came a fire, but the Lord was not in the fire. And after the fire came a gentle whisper. When Elijah heard it, he pulled his cloak over his face and went out and stood at the mouth of the cave. Then a voice said to him, "What are you doing here, Elijah?" He replied, "I have been very zealous for the Lord God Almighty. The Israelites have rejected Your covenant, broken down Your altars, and put Your prophets to death with the sword. I am the only one left, and now they are trying to kill me too" (1 Kings 19:8-14 NIV).

Just before this section of First Kings, Elijah had come from a big day on Mount Carmel. The Lord had really demonstrated His power by sucking up all the water with the fire. He had answered the challenge of the false prophets who were crying out for their false gods. Elijah said that the God who answered by fire was the one they were going to serve. So, the prophets of Baal called on their gods as they ritually cut themselves. Maybe their gods were on vacation, but who wants a god who takes a vacation? Just when you need him most, he is getting a suntan on the beach somewhere. When they had finished crying out to their gods, the God of Elijah answered with fire. Elijah had not forgotten the times God had demonstrated His power. He could rely on God.

What then, after you have had a great experience of victory? What are you going to do when it starts raining in your life? Some people say it's raining in their lives now. You really have to trust in God to survive. God will always be there with a still small voice after your Mount Carmel experience. After you have had your mountaintop experience and you are tested, God will be there to speak to you in a still small voice. He'll be there.

You tend to forget how God brought you through your last problem. Only yesterday God gave you a mountaintop experience, but you have already forgotten it. Sunday you were rejoicing and praising God. Then, on Monday you had the blues. You wonder, "What's going on here?" Tuesday you got depressed. Wednesday you were frustrated with something. Thursday it looked like the job was full of chaos and you hoped you could get through the week. If only you could make it to Friday. When Friday came, your paycheck wasn't what you thought it was going to be. Saturday you were bombarded by negative phone calls and you said, "Let me get to church Sunday morning because I don't know what I'm going to do if I don't get something to lean on."

The person you need to lean on is the one with the still small voice that was calling to you all week, but you were not listening to it. The still small voice is saying to you, "Lo, I am with you always, even unto the end of the world..." (see Mt. 28:20b). At the time of victory, right after your mountaintop experience, you didn't think you would be faced with another obstacle.

Jesus faced obstacles every day. Immediately following His baptism, our Lord faced the temptations of the devil. When you get out of church Sunday night, look out. You've praised the Lord, testified, and enjoyed the fellowship of the Holy Ghost. Watch out when you get up and testify or give a praise report. The devil is standing right outside the door waiting to attack you and destroy your joy. You must fortify your mind and determine to hold on to your good report.

In Second Corinthians 12, Paul is taken up to the third heaven. When he returns from all the splendor, we find him lamenting about a thorn in his flesh. The thorn in his flesh was a messenger sent by satan to buffet him. We don't know what the thorn represented, but the Lord didn't take it away. He asked God to take it away, but the Lord said to him, "My grace is sufficient." There are some things you'll never get over in this world. I don't care how much faith you have, there are things you will have to deal with the rest of your life. That does not mean God is not good or that God does not care about you. His grace is sufficient.

There are some things that may never get worked out as you would like them to. We ought to stop telling people everything will always be wonderful. If you call on God, He'll make the way. He will make the way, but there are some ways that won't be made. What are you going to do then? Are you going to trust God when the door closes, never to open again? Are you going to trust God if you lose a child who will never come to Christ? Are you going to trust God if your spouse is never saved? Will you trust God then?

A lot of people are following God for the goodies. As long as they are being blessed, or as long as they have a wonderful job, or as long as they have a beautiful relationship, or as long as their children are in college, they praise the Lord. While they have a fine automobile and a nice house, they praise the Lord. But as soon as the bottom falls out, they quit coming to church. You call them up and say, "Where have you been?" "Well, I'm just so discouraged; I don't know what's happening," they reply. You better make up your mind today that you don't serve God for the houses and land, but for who He is. If He never does anything else for you, He's still a good God.

Jesus went through temptations and Paul had a thorn in his flesh. Right after you return from your Mount Carmel experience, you must be prepared for an attack from the enemy. You must be particularly aware of subtle changes that, on the surface, seem of no consequence, but that may become more troublesome the longer you put them off.

In First Kings 19, Jezebel threatened Elijah. His nerves had gone into a tailspin and under the juniper tree he imagined that he was the only surviving saint, the last good man left in town. There are three great chapters in the life of this prophet and each might well be titled "Cheer Up, and Cave In." In the cave the Lord asked Elijah what he was doing in there. God wanted to know why he, the man of God, was in this cave. God might as well be saying, "What are you doing, people of God, in a cave of self-pity? Why do you insist on having a pity party?" You think no one knows what you are going through. If only someone knew your plight. You see the pastor and hear him preaching, but he doesn't know what you are going through.

It's amazing that people think the pastor and his family are immune to attack. Somehow God has put a little protective shield around them and they don't suffer or experience difficulties in their lives. They think that the anointed words just flow from his mouth so easily, that he couldn't possibly have any problems. What you may not realize is the pastor has the same day to face that you face. He is hit from every side, just as you are. The same devil who shoots at him also shoots at you. But the pastor has learned to praise instead of whine and cry.

You must learn to praise God in spite of what you are going through. I've asked the Lord, "Why me?" He said, "Why not you? You are just as good as anybody else to take this. Just because you're saved, filled with the Holy Ghost, speak in tongues, and prophesy, so what? That does not exempt you from the human experience of suffering. In this world you shall have trouble. Many are the afflictions of the righteous, but I will deliver you out of them all."

Just a few days ago I was thinking, "The sun is going to shine. I've been through so much; I just know I am about to break through and the sun is going to shine." Then, Pow! and here comes the devil again. Yet God's grace is still sufficient. Somebody asked me, "How do you make it?" I said, "I'm not making it; God is making it for me." A few of you saints are in the cave and you need to face the problem that has you hiding there.

Elijah was in the cave because he was tired. Many of God's people are tired too—especially those of us who have been in Church a long time. We have been bombarded with all kinds of problems and we have to deal with all types of attitudes. I'm not talking about outside the Church. I'm talking about in the Church. You try to do a good work and someone gets in the way.

Then you have these people with ego, who try to run everything. They put people in their places and they talk as if the Church was their personal property. They don't realize that the Church belongs to all of God's people. They try to undermine the pastor's authority and they use the pastor's name to achieve their own ends. If they aren't saying that the pastor told them, they are saying that God told them. If you want to know what the pastor said, ask the pastor. If you want to know what God said, ask God.

Thank God for His grace and the indwelling Holy Ghost. If it wasn't for His presence and His power, I would leave the church and never look back.

One of the problems I face in my church is the existence of cliques. If you are in the clique, the clique supports you. Cliques make signals in the church. They come to church and make signals and gestures and think I don't see them. I may not say anything, but you can be sure I am watching and I know where they are and what they are doing. Furthermore, I can read their spirits. What mother and father doesn't know their children? God won't put anyone in charge of a ministry unless he is in tune spiritually with His purpose and plan.

The cliques think they run things in their territories. The cliques seldom contribute financially. They elbow you and keep you out of the picture. They are trying to get the credit. If they were sincere, they would not be concerned about getting credit. A sincere person will exercise his ministry with a pure heart and his only concern will be to contribute to God's plan and purpose for the whole group. My advice to you is to be not weary in well doing. You shall reap if you faint not. (See Galatians 6:9.) God sees your labor of love and He will not forget what you are doing in your ministry (see Heb. 6:10). He'll give you the grace and strength to endure it.

God didn't rebuke Elijah for being tired. He fed him. The Bible tells us that He told him the journey was too great for Elijah and He gave him rest (see 1 Kings 19:7). The journey is too long for most of us these days. Never have I preached to so many tired people as I preach to now, all over this country. The human race lives in a state of nervous breakdown. It's a day of stress, a day of strain, a day of tension, and our speeches are the speech of weariness and the language of languor. We are weary and faint in our minds. Fatigue is filling the hospitals. Men cannot drink it away with whiskey; play it away at the card tables; laugh it away at a theater; or sleep it away with sedatives. Our remedies treat only the symptoms and not the disease.

A lady was asked, after being hurt in an automobile wreck, why she didn't sue for damages. She replied, "I got enough damages. All I need are some repairs." She was stating our case today. What we need are repairs.

The journey is too great even for our saints. The prophet speaks to edification, exhortation, and encouragement. He strengthens, stirs, and soothes. The saints need all three of them. We are to grow in grace and growth involves food, rest, and exercise. A lot of you need to take care of your physical body. You must take care of this body if you want it to be God's temple. You must take care of it so it will be strong, healthy, and fit for His use. You must eat the right food and you need adequate rest.

Some people have no consideration and because they can't sleep, they want to wake you up. They tell you that you were on their minds. If I'm on your mind, pray for me and leave me alone till the morning.

We also need to exercise. Instead of riding everywhere, find a way to exercise. The older people used to walk, walk, and walk. We should learn from their example. Now we act like walking is a fad. If you don't exercise, your body will just go out on you. In a few years you won't be able to use it at all.

Some eat the Word all the time and they need to exercise and work off some of the sermons they have stuffed themselves with. I'm talking about spiritual exercise now. You don't witness to others about Christ and you're not giving any praise reports. You just eat at the spiritual trough and sit down. You can come to church on Sunday morning, attend Bible class, and take in the Wednesday night faith-building clinic, but if you don't witness, if you don't win souls for Jesus Christ, you're going to be a bored saint. The Bible teaches us that we should witness. God feeds us so we can develop spiritually and so we can win others to Christ Jesus.

The Bible has as much to say about resting as it does about working. We need to set time aside and rest a while. If we don't take time to rest, we will come apart completely. We'll go to pieces. It's true that the enemy never takes a vacation, but we're not to follow the enemy. Jesus was never in a hurry. We need to learn the gait of Galilee. John Wesley said, "I do not have time to be in a hurry." Some saints tear around until you think the world would go to pieces if they stopped. Soon they blow their fuses and end up in the hospital because they don't slow down and rest in Christ. They go up like rockets and fall back down like rocks. They would do more if they did less. Quantity production is an American standard, not a Bible standard. All of us need to recognize that God is looking for us to move in a restful spirit.

"Come unto Me, all ye that labour and are heavy laden, and I will give you rest" (Mt. 11:28 KJV). This rest is not found in a graveyard. God wants you to get into a spirit of rest. He wants you to move in a spirit of confidence. He wants you to move in a spirit of trust, trusting God with your life. Give your life over to Him and let Him direct you.

Elijah was in the cave and he was thinking he was the only one left. It is a mistake to think we are the only saints left. Some of us in the Cathedral of Faith Church of God in Christ think there is nobody but us. But there is a whole army of people in churches all over the world who are saved and born again. They are with us, not against us. They are a part of God's Church here on earth.

God always has somebody waiting in the wings to do what you won't do. If you don't do what God gives you to do, God will take it and give it to somebody else. His will and purpose will be accomplished.

That's why, every time God speaks, you ought to move.

God told Elijah to go out, stand on the mountain, and wait for the Lord to pass by. There's some times we have to get into the presence of God to be revived, to be restored, because the soul gets discouraged. We need to recognize that we are in the presence of God so He can send His ministering angels to minister to us. How many of you know there are angels around you? How many of you know they are ministering to you? Often when people can't encourage you, or when you don't want to call anyone, the Lord has angels around you to minister to you. The reason you recover so quickly is because of these angels.

The Lord passed by Elijah not as a great wind that broke the rocks into pieces, or an earthquake or fire. He came to Elijah as a still small voice, a gentle whisper. When Elijah heard the voice of God, he pulled his cloak over his face and went out and stood at the mouth of the cave. When the Lord comes by, you will have to come out of the cave. When the Lord ministers to you, you will have to come out of that pity party. You will have to come out of the doubting dungeon.

Just the other day the Lord made Himself known to me. I said, "Thank You, Father." When the Lord ministers to you, it's like you've never been through a storm. The Lord asked Elijah why he was there. He replied, "I have been very jealous for the Lord God of hosts: for the children of Israel have forsaken Thy covenant, thrown down Thine altars, and slain Thy prophets with the sword; and I, even I only, am left; and they seek my life, to take it away" (1 Kings 19:10).

Actually, the Lord had seven thousand people who had not bowed to the false god, Baal. There are born-again people who you don't know about because they have never bowed down. That's why we should hold up the standard for the King. Let the world know that nothing can get you down and keep you down.

You don't know what tomorrow is going to bring. You never know what's up the road. You never know what you have to endure. You never know how many things will be thrown at you. But if you have the assurance, if you learn how to trust God, then God will help you. The Spirit spoke to me and said, "Every one of My children has to learn how to trust Me because this is a trying time for the saints. It's not going to be easy from here on."

For the 1990's, the enemy has mustered his forces. They are all fired up and demonic forces have never been stronger. They are on the attack and after the saints. Demonic activity and witchcraft are on the increase. Satan worship is increasing among African-Americans. Intelligent young people, who should know better, are practicing satanism. Even people in the church are involved in witchcraft. If you truly know Christ Jesus, you will never be involved in satanic practices. Many come to church professing Jesus, but many don't have the Holy Ghost. Many are talking about Jesus, but they don't know Jesus because they are into devil worship, voodooism, and fortune tellers. They are reading tarot cards and living their lives according to their astrological signs.

I don't talk about those signs. I'm only talking about the signs Jesus told us about. He said that signs would follow those who believe; in His name they would cast out devils (see Mk. 16:17). I don't care if you're a Cancer, a Gemini, or a Leo. Are you a child of God? If you're a child of God, you don't need to read the newspaper to see what you should do today. Acknowledge God and He'll direct your path (see Prov. 3:6). We see so much of this Ouija board activity. Are you going to a Ouija board to get your answer? You should go to your knees in prayer. God has the answer. Satan knows the time is short and he's getting into the church and into your leadership. I don't want a spiritualist giving me a word. I want my word to come from the Lord. Are you asking just anyone for a word from the Lord? What do they tell you? Do they tell you what you want to hear? Do they see good luck for you? Luck has nothing to do with it. If you will only listen to the still small voice, all those other voices that are clogging your mind will fade out of earshot. You will be free to praise the Lord, dance in the spirit, and sing your songs of gladness. You can testify with a good report. You can hear and understand the preaching and teaching of the Word.

After the doors close, after the maintenance people lock the doors and the lights are out, you will go out into the world. There the enemy is roaming about seeking to devour, to destroy, to kill, and to steal (see 1 Pet. 5:8; Jn. 10:10). He wants to kill your spirit and steal your joy. What are you going to do? You better have the Lord inside you. You better know Him for yourself. You better know that you can trust Him so you can deal with things. In the face of danger, in the face of trouble, you need to hear that still small voice saying, "I'm with you. My grace is sufficient. Rest in Me. Wait patiently for Me. Delight yourself in Me. I'll give you the desires of your heart. I'm your light and your salvation. Whom shall ye fear? I'm your Shepherd; you shall not want. Dwell in Me, the secret place of the most high."

Chapter 11

God Causes You to Triumph

"Now thanks be unto God, which always causeth us to triumph in Christ..." (2 Cor. 2:14a KJV). We are more than conquerors through Jesus Christ, and God always causes us to triumph. Another version says it like this: "But thanks be to God! For through what Christ has done, He has triumphed over us so that now wherever we go He uses us to tell others about the Lord and to spread the Gospel like a sweet perfume" (2 Cor. 2:14).

We are to give glory to God when we triumph. Through all the trials and tribulations, God alone receives glory. God gets His greatest victories out of apparent defeats. Very often the enemy seems to triumph for a time. God allows it sometimes. But then God comes in and upsets all the work of the enemy, overthrows the apparent victory, and as the Bible says, "turns the way of the wicked upside down" (see Ps. 146:9). What the devil intends for evil, God turns around for good.

I said to my daughter, "You know, some things, if taken in isolation, seem evil through our eyes and our understanding." Through our finite thinking they appear as negative and it seems like we face defeat. But every one of us must learn this one principle: All things work together for good to them that love God, to the called according to His purpose. (See Romans 8:28.) We must understand that God allows a lot of things to happen in our lives just to get us to a particular place in Him. Life seems to be filled with things that we think are not supposed to happen. It may surprise us, but God is never caught by surprise. God knows what will happen before it begins and He has enough grace to sustain us and to keep us stable in the midst of an unstable situation.

In Judges 6 and 7, Gideon is faced with certain defeat at the hands of the Midianites and Amalekites. He started out with an army of 32,000, but the Lord said there were too many. In the natural, the more you have, the better the chance of success. Nevertheless, God told all of those who were fearful and afraid to leave. Twenty-two thousand left and 10,000 remained. Still, according to the Lord's measure, there were too many. So Gideon had them go to the river and told them to take a drink of water. Only those who lapped the water from his hand would be allowed to remain. Nine thousand seven hundred returned home and Gideon was left with an army of only 300 to face the forces of both of the opposing nations.

It looked as if the servants of the living God were going to have a terrible defeat; they would certainly fall at the hands of such a formidable force. Surely the enemy would prevail. We can imagine what must have been going through Gideon's mind. The Lord can put you in a situation where things seem hopeless. What might have disastrous consequences will not affect those who are under orders from God.

Just as God delivered the Hebrew boys from the fiery furnace, He delivered Gideon and the people of Israel from the hands of a superior force. He knows exactly how to fight the battle and He knows exactly how many soldiers are needed to achieve victory. We don't have to question God. The Lord can take the weight out of the load. He gives you the opportunity to win and He expects you to act responsibly. He replaces the apparent overwhelming odds with His strength, and His grace is more than enough to make up for any weakness you may have.

The grace of God will sustain you in any situation. Suppose Gideon and his band of 300 had lost their faith and courage. Suppose he had complained, "Why don't You call back the whole army to help us? Why did You put us in this predicament?" I have heard a lot of saints complain, "Why does God allow me to go through this when I serve Him with all my heart and I do what I can for Him? I'm going to church and I'm paying my tithes, and I'm doing this and that. Why do I see wicked people prospering?" The Bible tells us not to fret because of evildoers who prosper in their ways. They will be cut down as the grass and wither as the green herb (see Ps. 37:1-2). There are people who don't even care about God and seem to be getting along much better than you are. But you don't understand. Unlike them, God is with you and He's going to take care of you in your situation.

Have you ridden a bicycle lately? It's not too difficult to go downhill on a bicycle. You can coast when going down a hill. But you try going up a steep hill and you have to labor because of the weight. You're going to feel the pull on your legs. It's not too bad to go down steps, but try running up steps. When you get to the top you have to stop for a while, take hold of the banister, and wait to get your breath.

It's not too difficult to be a sinner. It's not too difficult to have fun, enjoy yourself, and be on the enemy's side. It's not too difficult to go downhill, downhill to the world of destruction, but when you start walking up the highway, the King's highway, walking upright before God, it is often difficult.

The enemy doesn't want you to live for God and surrender your will to God. He will oppose you at every opportunity. How many of you feel like you've been in a civil war since you've been saved? Do you feel like you are facing a force that seems to be without number? You're constantly battling, constantly trying to do what God says, and the old self keeps saying, "I want to have my way." The Bible tells us that we have a war going on (see Rom. 7:23). You have to decide if you are going to let Jesus be Lord of your life. You have to make the decision to crucify the flesh and you will have to die daily to the cares and the pleasures of this life.

God took certain defeat before the mighty forces of two nations and turned it to victory with a force of only 300 soldiers. Gideon is a type of Christ, a leader in the army of God. Jesus said, "I will never leave you nor will I forsake you. I'll go with you all the way even unto the end of the world" (see Heb. 13:5; Mt. 28:20). Whatever you're going through right now, the Lord is with you. He gives you the victory to triumph in Christ. If there's a great trial in your life today, don't accept defeat. Continue in faith and claim the victory through Him who is able to make you more than a conqueror. Your victory is at hand.

Every battle is a chance for victory and every victory is a chance to give the glory to the Lord. Many are the afflictions of the righteous, but God delivers us out of them all (see Ps. 34:19). God is sustaining you right now. He is causing you to triumph in the midst of all that you are going through, whether it is a fiery furnace or an insurmountable battle.

In the world you don't get the victories that I'm talking about. In the human arena, things that seem to be defeats are not defeats in the spiritual arena. What seems to be evil in the natural arena is not evil in the spiritual arena. In the spiritual arena, everything that comes upon us is a test God allows us to take. When we go through these things, we learn how to trust God and to put Him first in our lives. We also learn that God sustains us and that, through it all, we are being developed in the Lord.

Like the process of crushing flowers to make perfume, we have to be crushed to start the process. Then, when the oil of the Spirit is mixed in, we become a full fragrance. God takes His saints and allows satan to crush them because He has invested His Spirit in them and He's joined them with the sweet-smelling fragrance of the Savior. When He gets through allowing the enemy to crush you, and then mixing you Himself with the oil of anointing, you come out smelling like Jesus. Now you are ready to go into all the world and spread that fragrance. You came through the trials, tribulations, and persecutions and in the soil of God's making, you became a precious perfume.

This book comes out of my being crushed and out of my being persecuted. But God will get the glory out of it. Do you notice how many testimonies you have that at first seemed like defeats? Instead they turn out to be victories. When the battle starts, you say, "Oh God, now this. No, not this happening to me. No, Lord, I don't want to go through this." Then after it is over, you realize you have a testimony of victory and a praise report to offer to God. You were able to tell everyone, "Listen, God brought me through a terrible battle and He has done great things for me." When it was all over, you even loved God a little bit more.

Through these trying experiences, you learn to appreciate Him more. You learn how to walk in Him with joy in your heart. You've come a long way; you've been in the fiery furnace; you've been in the lion's den; you've been through the valley; but when the devil thought he had you down, God raised you up.

I like the traditional song *Victory Shall Be Mine* that the old-timers used to sing: "Victory, victory shall be mine. If I hold my peace and let the Lord fight my battle, victory shall be mine." All you have to do is wait on God and patiently look to Him, the Author and Finisher of your faith (see Heb. 12:2). The devil shot SCUD missiles at me and he's continued to send scud missiles my way. Hussein wasn't shooting at me; it was the devil. He is still trying to hit me with one of his evil missiles, but God has a shield around me and around His saints and whatever the enemy sends our way will be of no effect. It can shake you up sometimes and may cause you to get discouraged. It can sometimes cause you to go through a state of depression, but God will not let the devil destroy His saints. Those who love God can relax in God and say, "This too will pass away."

I hear somebody saying, "But oh, Pastor Greer, you don't know what I'm up against today." I want you to know that whatever you are up against can't destroy you. I want you to know that God always causes you to triumph. You can't get this victory on your own. You can't overcome the devil on our own. Only God's hand can lift you up and bring you out of your battle victorious.

There are times when God, in His mercy, says, "Enough! The enemy has plagued you long enough and you have fought the best you know how. He thinks he is about to get his way, but I have seen your plight and I will put a stop to him now." At other times, God expects you to stand up to the enemy and, like Jesus, say, "Satan, I'm sick and tired of you now. I rebuke you and resist you in the name of Jesus." The Bible tells us that when we resist the evil one, he must flee from us (see Jas. 4:7).

God causes us to triumph over all of these circumstances. The saints can come to church and praise the Lord and still be hit from every side. But they don't have to sit in the corner and have a pity party. They should walk in the sanctuary praising God. The world doesn't understand how can you praise God like that. They don't understand how you can go to church when your whole world is crumbling around you. They don't realize your help comes from the Lord.

All of your strength comes from God. All of your joy comes from the Lord and the joy of the Lord is your strength (see Neh. 8:10). I would have fainted unless I had believed to see the goodness of the Lord in the land of the living. Yes, you could have fainted last week, but God caused you to triumph over all of that. The Lord causes you to triumph in Christ Jesus. You're more than a conqueror. God wants His people to praise Him now more than they've ever praised Him before. He doesn't want us to complain. Instead He wants to change our vocabulary to start thanking Jesus. Thank Him for bringing you through; thank Him for keeping you safe; and thank Him for preparing a way for you to follow Him through the next obstacle.

If the Lord brought you this far, He can take you on. He causes you to triumph over and over again. You get victory after victory until you finally get to that place where you can say you have learned how to be content in whatever state you are in. You are not going to let your burdens get you down. You are not going to let your problems get you down. You are not going to let circumstances get you down. You choose to praise the Lord and you are not going to let one day go by without praising the Lord. Praise Him in the morning, praise Him in the noonday, praise Him in the evening. Thank Him for everything. With every breath you take, praise the Lord, for the more you praise Him, the more you will be victorious. The more you praise Him, the better you will feel.

If this concept of the Lord's causing you to triumph would hit all of the saints, nothing would be able to stand in our way. It isn't by your own will that you overcome or by your own effort that you reach the heights. It is by God's action in and through you that you are able to shout praises and to claim the victory. When you understand the source of your power, you will come to rely only on that source and none other.

This is where He wants to lead the saints of today. He wants the Church to be more aggressive spiritually and to learn from past generations. We have a lot to be thankful for in the past, but God doesn't want us to live in the eighteenth century any more. The saints of the twenty-first century are poised to move into another dimension. That includes those of us who realize we have the power of God to overcome and we're greater than any enemy who tries to come against us. As conquerors through Christ Jesus, we have a mandate to bring His Kingdom to the forefront.

Although you live in the world, you are not of the world. You don't have to react like the world reacts because you are not subject to panic attacks. When you abandon your concern for worldly things, you don't lose anything; rather, you gain the opportunity to do something else for God. When you've overcome the world, the loss of house or car or job is nothing because you live in abundance when you live with God. You can continue to lift your voice in praise, for you know the earth is the Lord's and the fullness thereof (see 1 Cor. 10:26).

In order to truly benefit as an overcomer, you must exercise your overcoming spirit through practice. You no longer react to sickness like the world reacts to sickness. You'll say, "My body is the temple of the Holy Ghost. My body belongs to the Lord. He can do what He wants with it. By His stripes I'm healed and I refuse to say I'm sick. I am well, not sick; strong, not weak; rich, not poor. I am rich through Christ Jesus who causes me to triumph over this world's cares. Even though I am a resident of the world, I am not of this world. My principles are Kingdom principles, so I am not bound by worldly principles. From this point on I will use the divine Kingdom principles—spiritual principles—that govern the spiritual laws I walk in."

So no matter what you are facing in life today, continue to praise your God. Be free in Him; rest in Him. Don't let troubles get you down. Hold on for that miracle. Focus on God and who He is. Begin to praise Him right now!

Appendix

Praise Reports From Cathedral of Faith Church

All over the world people are standing to testify to the goodness and mercy of God as He works in and through their lives. The same is true at my church and with the members of my congregation. Now that you know how important it is to be free, you should also know that the process of acknowledging God in your life will produce results. The following testimonies—we call them praise reports—are compiled from actual transcripts from the lives of real people. They were given at various times during our church services. I want to share them with you so you can read the accounts yourself.

Sister Valerie

Praise the Lord. I am happy to be here again. During the Fourth of July weekend, I met with Pastor Greer and told him about a struggle that I was having with a call on my life to minister the Lord's Word. I went to a Kenneth Hagin crusade and when I came back, the devil tried to hinder me. I had gotten it in my spirit that I was going to get some news. I didn't know if it was good news or bad news, I only knew it was news. I began to pray and ask the Lord to help me receive it. On a Monday morning, about 4 a.m., the phone rang and it was the nurse from my doctor's office. She told me, in examining a test I had taken, that they had found a cancer. I had battled cancer some years ago, so I began to say, "You know, Lord"—I began to rebuke it in my spirit, and I just said, "Lord, You know I received deliverance in 1979. I am not going to start asking You over again in 1991. I am going to stand and hold onto that 1979 deliverance."

So, I just started standing fast. I got quiet, went through some more changes, but I started saying, "I am not going to clothe myself in cancer. I am not going to clothe myself in things that the devil wants to give me. I am going to put on the whole armor of the Lord, and I am going to fight the good fight of faith." It is a good fight that we are fighting. So, I went on and I did as the doctor told me. I went through biopsies and the lab work. I started taking medication, even though, in my spirit, I wouldn't receive the cancer. When I went to have surgery, my doctor said, "You know, Val, everything looks like it's going to be okay." I said, "Praise You, Jesus. I just thank You, Lord. Hallelujah! Thank You, Jesus. Hallelujah! Thank You, Lord. Glory to God."

That's my testimony, but I want to share this. I said, "Lord, why do I have to go through this, or if I went through it one time, why do I have to go through it again?" He said, "Valerie, Jesus had to bear the sickness, poverty, sins, and diseases, and He did that for all. People who have been called, who have been given much, from them much is required." We have to bear the infirmities so we can come back and tell others that God is able to keep them from falling. We have to bear sickness, sins, and diseases, so we can say that God is the deliverer. So I am here and I went through all of that so someone wouldn't have to go through it. I am here to tell others that I don't care about AIDS, I don't care about cancer, I don't care about diabetes, I don't care about lupus, I don't care about leukemia. Don't clothe yourself in any of these. God didn't give these to you, so don't take them. We don't have to take anything—glory—the devil gives us.

God told me that while I was going through this, it was a cleansing. I told the Lord that things were happening and that I didn't have time to be sick. I said, "Lord, what must I do?" and I began to cry out. He said, "Honey, it ain't no playing you're going through. You have to go through that thing all by yourself—you and Jesus." Glory to God!

I said, "Lord, what do You want me to do?"

He said, "Val, I want you to lay aside every heavy weight" and He started putting people in my mind.

He showed me sins that I was carrying. You know, no one is perfect. I'd be the first to confess.

He said, "Val, lay some of this aside and lay some of these people aside and lay all these things that are hindering you aside and you just go on. If you have to go on by yourself, Val, go on." He said, "My yoke is easy; My burden is light."

I was burdened. I can't tell you my pain, having to go through this sickness, having faith, trying to have faith. I can't tell you about it. My friends were calling me, telling me their problems, and I had to keep my mouth closed and be a minister to them.

I said, "Lord, it's the life that's standing here to be called a minister. I don't desire to be this thing, but if it's Your will, Lord, I'll do it." Whatever it is that the Lord wants me to do, I'll do it. We don't have to take anything. That is the essence. That is the message. We don't have to take anything. We don't have to clothe ourselves in anything that the devil gives us because he is not our father. I only receive from my Father.

Sister Mary Goodwin

I had a heart attack in 1987. Then in June 1992, I had another heart attack. The doctor said that every heart attack is bad. There is no little heart attack and no big heart attack. But, the Lord brought me through.

It has been two-and-a-half months and I was planning to go back to California to get my furniture and my car, but the internist said, "Oh, no. You can forget about that. You're not going anywhere."

But, I called my doctor. Then my cardiologist called back and said, "Your heart is healed. It's healed. You can travel." The last time he gave me an echocardiogram, he kept pushing that thing all over my chest, saying, "This is something! You're lucky, you're really lucky. Your heart is stronger now than it was when you had the last heart attack in 1987." He said, "I can't believe this. I can't believe this—you're lucky!"

I said, "No, no, I am blessed. I am blessed of the Lord, for I am not supposed to be running around here. I'm not supposed to be jumping up and down and going on. I'm supposed to be walking around all pitiful and heart-damaged, with my muscles all broken down so I can hardly breathe. I'm not supposed to be strong like this."

Many say there is too much on me. They say that I am doing too much. But you know what? Daily, God loads me with benefits. God gives me strength. I believe it is because I consider the poor. I believe it's because I work for the Lord, because I am committed to Him, dedicated to Him and His little ones in Haiti. I'm just simple enough to believe that. I believe that it works because God promised me if I would take care of His business, He would take care of mine and He would take care of me. I'm here to tell anybody that is hedging away from doing what God would have them to do, to step out and God will take care of you. You wouldn't believe what I came back to when I came back from California. My poor body couldn't take it, but my spirit took it. God let me know that His grace was sufficient and He is bringing me out. It is not all over yet. Everything's not finished. Everything is not together. I'm still having problems, but God is lifting me while I'm yet under the load. Hallelujah!

He will do that for you. He will make you strong. He will help you to go through because His grace is sufficient. I thank God, because I am glad I know Him. I wouldn't be anywhere else but here. I love the Lord for He heard my cry. He pitied every groan. He has been a shelter for me.

Deacon James McWhorter, Sr.

Since my retirement a year ago, I have been a little depressed. My thoughts have been filled with worry. I tried not to focus on my worries by walking around the house and thanking God for His work in and through my life, but I couldn't get my mind to settle down. So, I went out in the yard to finish a small job I had started, thinking this would distract my thoughts. But the Lord continued to deal with me and I couldn't get away from the things He was bringing into my mind. Later that evening, I retired early, but it was after 12 o'clock before I went to sleep. The next morning I looked like satan had tried to do me in.

The way I looked and felt reminded me of my childhood in the country. Satan began to bring up memories of my childhood. I began to remember the deep wells we had throughout the area. I don't know how they were able to dig the wells so deep. Some were reportedly 180 feet deep. I had even helped dig a well, but we never had to go any deeper than 30 feet. I also remembered the water in the bottom of the wells, so clear and cool.

Suddenly, I remembered the time one of my uncle's little children almost fell over backwards into the well. The well was boxed in and the child was sitting on the edge, near the bucket. The memory of that deep well made me think satan was trying to carry me down into a deep gulf. I had the vision of falling, and falling, going down and down. It seemed as if he was trying to get me down into one of those wells. I started rebuking him, saying, "Devil, you lie, you lie. You are not going to take my mind and get me to doing something or another and fall into this well." At that moment Pastor Greer appeared and I said, "I'm going to fall into this well," but the pastor said, "No, don't give in. Say don't—not yet; say, not yet." I told Pastor Greer that if I can get down yonder, I can conquer this devil. He said, "No, Brother McWhorter, say 'not yet.'" And I was obedient to the voice of my pastor.

After a while he said, "Now step out." And when I stepped out, I stepped out in the name of Jesus. The trust that I had in my pastor helped me walk right by the enemy. As I walked by, the enemy drew back and ran. The more he turned back, the bolder I got and I began to walk with my chest out.

I have been through a lot in my lifetime. I don't talk much, I don't tell all of the things I have been through. But I want you to know that the Lord has been good to me. He's saved my life many, many times. I just thank God for His protection.

We all need to do more with our lives, as the pastor told us recently. As saints we need to do something that we can thank God for. We say we are saved and, if that is true, we need to join hands and go out and conquer Atlanta, Georgia, for the Lord. We need to get out in the streets and deal with some of these folks who don't know the Lord. You'll be surprised what you can do and the way they will respond to you. They'll throw their arms around you because they have been waiting for the love of God to be offered to them. They want to hear something. They want somebody to tell them that they are loved. Love is what God is all about.

I don't care who you are. If you mistreat me, I ask Him to forgive me for it and forgive you. I forgive you, but my dealing with you will be shorter from then on because He said know them that labor among you and watch and pray. That's what I do, I watch and pray. What I'm dealing with right now in the spirit are the words we will all hear. When we enter the final kingdom, He will ask us about our brothers and our sisters. We are supposed to help our brothers and

Appendix

our sisters. God deals with me about the people in my neighborhood. I encourage them to go to church and many of them come with me. Each Sunday morning I consider it my job to come to church and I enjoy my work. There is no other place I would rather be than in this church.

I can do all things through Christ which strengtheneth me (Philippians 4:13).

Overcoming Spiritual Mediocrity by Jonathan Greer II contains a message that will both encourage and challenge you. Learn how to be a "can do" saint and to take a bold approach for making the impossible...possible.

To order *Overcoming Spiritual Mediocrity* by Dr. Jonathan Greer II, send $6.95 for each copy ordered to:

Cathedral of Faith Church of God in Christ
1137 Avon Avenue, S.W.
Atlanta, GA 30310